D0976560

CONNECTING IN JESUS

6 SMALL GROUP
SESSIONS ON
FELLOWSHIP

STUDENT EDITION

DOUG FIELDS &
BRETT EASTMAN

ZONDERVAN™

GRAND RAPIDS, MICHIGAN 49530 USA

ZONDERVAN.COM/
AUTHOR**TRACKER**

Youth Specialties

www.youthspecialties.com

Youth Specialties

Connecting in Jesus, Student Edition: Six Sessions on Fellowship
Copyright © 2006 by Doug Fields and Brett Eastman

Youth Specialties products, 300 South Pierce Street, El Cajon, CA 92020, are published by Zondervan, 5300 Patterson Avenue SE, Grand Rapids, MI 49530

Library of Congress Cataloging-in-Publication Data

Fields, Doug, 1962-
     Connecting in Jesus : six sessions on fellowship / Doug Fields and Brett Eastman.
         p. cm. -- (Experiencing Christ together, student edition)
     Includes bibliographical references and index.
     ISBN-10: 0-310-26645-9 (pbk. : alk. paper)
     ISBN-13: 978-0-310-26645-7 (pbk. : alk. paper)
     1. Fellowship--Biblical teaching. 2. Fellowship--Study and teaching.
I. Eastman, Brett, 1959-   . II. Title. III. Series: Fields, Doug, 1962-   .
Experiencing Christ together. Student edition.
     BV4517.5.F54 2006
     248.4'0715--dc22
                                                                        2005024172

Web site addresses listed in this book were current at the time of publication. Please contact Youth Specialties via e-mail (YS@YouthSpecialties.com) to report URLs that are no longer operational and replacement URLs if available.

Creative Team: Dave Urbanski, Holly Sharp, Mark Novelli, Joanne Heim, Janie Wilkerson
Cover Design: Mattson Creative
Printed in the United States of America

05 06 07 08 09 10 • 10 9 8 7 6 5 4 3 2 1

ACKNOWLEDGMENTS

This series of six books couldn't have happened if there weren't some wonderful friends who chimed in on the process and added their heart and level of expertise to these pages. I need to acknowledge and thank my friends for loving God, caring for students and supporting me-especially true on this task were Amanda Maguire, Nancy Varner, Ryanne Dearden, Jana Sarti, Matt McGill and the crew at Simply Youth Ministry. I sure appreciate doing life together. Also, I'm very appreciative of Brett Eastman for asking me to do this project.

TABLE OF CONTENTS

Introduction: Read Me First!   7

Small Group Covenant   17

Session 1   As I Have Loved You   19

Session 2   Love That Shows Up   31

Session 3   Loving Difficult People   41

Session 4   Truthful but Tender   51

Session 5   Extreme Forgiveness   61

Session 6   Cross-Shaped Love   73

Appendices   85

INTRODUCTION: READ ME FIRST!

Welcome to a Journey with Jesus (and Others)!

I hope you're ready for God to do something great in your life as you use this book and connect with a few friends and a loving small group leader. The potential of this combination is incredible. The reason we know its potential is that we've heard from thousands of students who've already gone through our first series of LIFETOGETHER books and shared their stories. We've been blessed to hear that the combination of friends gathering together, books with great questions, and the Bible as a foundation have provided the ingredients for life change. As you read these words, know that you're beginning a journey that may revolutionize your life.

The following six sessions are designed to help you grow in your knowledge of Jesus and his teachings and become his devoted disciple. But growth doesn't happen alone. You need God's help and a community of people who love God, too. We've found that a great way to grow strong in Christ is in the context of a caring spiritual community (or small group). This community is committed to doing life together—at least for a season—and will thrive when each small group member (you) focuses on Jesus as well as the others in the group.

This type of spiritual community isn't easy. It requires several things from you:

- trust
- confidentiality
- honesty
- care
- openness
- risk
- commitment to meet regularly

Anyone can meet with a few people and call it a group, but it takes stronger commitment and desire to create a spiritual community where others can know you, love you, care for you, and give you the freedom to open up about your thoughts, doubts, and struggles—a place where you're safe to be yourself.

We've learned from the small groups that didn't work that spiritual community can't develop without honesty. Now, at first you may be tempted to show up to your small group session and sit, smile, act nicely, and never speak from your heart—but this type of superficial participation prevents true spiritual community. Please fight through this temptation and know that when you reveal who you really are, you'll contribute something unique and powerful to the group that can't occur any other way. Your honest sharing about your heart and soul will challenge other group members to do the same, and they'll likely become as honest as you are.

To help you get to this place of honesty, every session contains questions that are intended to push you to think, talk, and open your heart. They'll challenge you to expose some of your fears, hurts, and habits. Through them, I guarantee you'll experience spiritual growth and relational intimacy, and you'll build lasting, genuine friendships.

All mature Christians will tell you that God used others to impact their lives. God has a way of allowing one life to connect with another to result in richer, deeper, and more vibrant lives for both. As you go through this book (and the five others in this series), you will have the opportunity to impact someone else—and someone else will have the opportunity to impact you. You'll both become deeper, stronger followers of Jesus Christ. So get ready for some life change.

WHO IS JESUS?

Most people have an opinion about Jesus. But many of these opinions are based on what they've heard or come up with on their own—what they'd *prefer* Jesus to be—as opposed to their own discovery of Jesus through the Bible. People believe Jesus was all kinds of things—a great teacher, a leader of a revolution, a radical with a political agenda, a gentle man with a big vision, a prophet, a spiritual person who emphasized religion. Still others believe he is who he claimed to be—God.

The Jesus of the Bible is far more compelling than most people's opinions about him. *Connecting in Jesus* allows you to get to know Jesus as his first followers did. They met Jesus as teacher, a rabbi. They came to know Jesus as healer, shepherd, servant, Savior, and ultimately the one who defeated death— the risen Lord. From his first words, "Follow me," through his ministry, death, and resurrection, he kept drawing people deeper into his life.

Jesus asked his disciples to commit their lives to God's way. As you read the Bible, you'll see that God's ways weren't always easy or comfortable for the disciples to follow. But what motivated them to do what he taught was their rich experience of who he was and all he did for them. *Connecting in Jesus* will ground you in that same experience so you'll more fully desire to follow Jesus and commit to his ways—even when it's not easy or comfortable. The Jesus you're about to encounter is waiting for you to meet him, get closer to him, and commit your life to following his ways and teachings.

When you align your life with Jesus, you're in for a wild, adventurous life. It won't be without its difficulties, but it'll be a better life than you ever dreamed possible.

WHAT YOU NEED TO KNOW ABOUT EACH OF THESE SIX SESSIONS

Each session in this study contains more material than you and your group can complete in a typical meeting of an hour or so. The key to making the most of each session is to choose which questions you'll answer and discuss and which ones you'll save for your alone time. We've tried to make it simple, so if you miss something from one meeting, you can pick it up the next time you're together. Let's be more specific.

Each of the six sessions in *Connecting in Jesus* contains five unique sections. These five sections have the same titles in every book and in every session in the LIFETOGETHER series. The sections are (1) fellowship, (2) discipleship, (3) ministry, (4) evangelism, and (5) worship. These represent five biblical purposes that we believe lead to personal spiritual growth, growth in your student ministry, and health for your entire church. The more you think about these five purposes and try to make them part of your life, the stronger you'll be and the more you'll grow spiritually.

While these five biblical purposes make sense individually, they can make a greater impact when they're brought together. Think of it in sports terms: if you play baseball or softball, you might be an outstanding hitter—but you also need to catch, throw, run, and slide. You need more than one skill to impact your team. In the same way, having a handle on one or two of the five biblical purposes is great—but when they're all reflected together in a person's life, that person is much more biblically balanced and healthy.

You'll find that the material in this book (and in the other LIFETOGETHER books) is built around the Bible. There are a lot of blank spaces and journaling pages where you can write down your thoughts about God's Word and God's work in your life as you explore and live out God's biblical purposes.

Each session begins with a short story that helps introduce the theme. If you have time to read it, great—if not, no big deal. Immediately following the story are five key sections. The following is a brief description of each:

♥ FELLOWSHIP: CONNECTING YOUR HEART TO OTHERS

Goal: To share about your life and listen attentively to others, caring about what they share

You'll begin your session with a few minutes of conversation that will give you all a chance to share from your own lives, get to know each other better, and offer initial thoughts about the session's theme. The icon for this section is a heart because you're opening up your heart so others can connect with you on a deeper level.

DISCIPLESHIP: GROWING TO BE LIKE JESUS

Goal: To explore God's Word, gain biblical knowledge, and make personal applications

This section will take the most time. You'll explore the Bible and gain some knowledge about Jesus. You'll encounter his life and teachings and discuss how God's Word can make a difference in your own life. The icon for this section is a brain because you're opening your mind to learn God's Word and his ways.

You'll find lots of questions in this section—more than you can discuss during your group time. Your leader will choose the questions you have time to discuss or come up with different questions. We encourage you to respond to the skipped questions on your own; during the week it's a great way to get more Bible study time.

MINISTRY: SERVING OTHERS IN LOVE

Goal: To recognize and take advantage of opportunities to serve others

When you get to this section, you'll have an opportunity to discuss how to express God's love through serving others. The discussion and opportunities are created to tie into the topic. As you grow spiritually, you'll naturally begin to recognize and take opportunities to serve others. As your heart grows, so will your opportunities to serve. Here, the icon is a foot because feet communicate movement and action—serving and meeting the needs of others requires you to act on what you've learned.

EVANGELISM: SHARING YOUR STORY AND GOD'S STORY

Goal: To consider how the truths from this session might be applied to your relationships with unbelievers

It's very easy for a small group to turn into a clique that only looks inward and loses sight of others outside the group. That's not God's plan. God wants you to reach out to people with his message of love and life change. While this is often scary, this section will give you an opportunity to discuss your relationships with non-Christians and consider ways to listen to their stories, share pieces of your story, and reflect the amazing love of God's story. The icon for this section is a mouth because you're opening your mouth to have spiritual conversations with nonbelievers.

WORSHIP: SURRENDERING YOUR LIFE TO HONOR GOD

Goal: To focus on God's presence

Each session ends with a time of prayer. You'll be challenged to slow down and turn your focus toward God's love, his goodness, and his presence in your life. You'll spend time talking to God, listening in silence, reading Scripture, writing, and focusing on God. The key word for this time is *surrender*, which is giving up what you want so God can give you what he wants. The icon for this section is a body, which represents surrendering your entire life to God.

Oh yeah...there are more sections in each session!

In addition to the main material, there are several additional options you can use to help further and deepen your times with God. Many people attend church programs, listen, and then "leave" God until the next week when they return to church. We don't want that to happen to you! So we've provided several more opportunities for you to learn, reflect, and grow on your own.

At the end of every session you'll find three more key headings:

- At Home This Week
- Learn a Little More
- For Deeper Study on Your Own

They're fairly easy to figure out, but here's a brief description of each:

AT HOME THIS WEEK

There are five options presented at the end of each session that you can do on your own. They're not homework for the next session (unless your leader assigns them to your group); they're things you can do to keep growing at your own pace. You can skip them, you can do all of them, or you can vary the options from session to session.

Option 1: A Weekly Reflection

At the end of each session you'll find a one-page, quick self-evaluation that helps you reflect on the five key areas of your spiritual life (fellowship, discipleship, ministry, evangelism, and worship). It's simply a guide for you to gauge your spiritual health. The first one is on page 29.

Option 2: Daily Bible Readings

One of the challenges in deepening your knowledge of God's Word and learning more about Jesus' life is to read the Bible on your own. This option provides a guide to help you read through the Gospel of Luke in 30 days. On pages 122-123 is a list of Bible passages to help you continue to take God's Word deeper into your life.

Option 3: Memory Verses

On pages 127-128 you'll find six Bible verses to memorize. Each is related to the theme of a particular session. (Again, these are optional…remember, nothing is mandatory!)

Option 4: Journaling

You'll find a question or two related to the theme of the session that can serve as a trigger to get you writing. Journaling is a great way to reflect on what you've been learning and evaluate your life. In addition to questions at the end of each session, there's a helpful tool on page 129 that can guide you through the discipline of journaling.

Option 5: Wrap It Up

As you've already read, each session contains too many questions for one small group meeting. So this section provides opportunities to think through your answers to the questions you skipped and then go back and write them down.

LEARN A LITTLE MORE

We've provided some insights (or commentary) on some of the passages that you'll study to help you understand the difficult terms, phrases, and people that you'll read about in each Bible passage.

FOR DEEPER STUDY ON YOUR OWN

One of the best ways to understand the Bible passages and the theme of each session is to dig a little deeper. If deeper study fits your personality style, please use these additional ideas as ways to enhance your learning.

WHAT YOU NEED TO KNOW ABOUT BEING IN A SMALL GROUP

You probably have enough casual or superficial friendships and don't need to waste your time cultivating more. We all need deep and committed friendships. Here are a few ideas to help you benefit the most from your small group time and build great relationships.

Prepare to Participate

Interaction is key to a good small group. Talking too little will make it hard for others to get to know you. Everyone has something to contribute—yes, even you! But participating doesn't mean dominating, so be careful not to monopolize the conversation. Most groups typically have one conversation hog, and if you don't know who it is in your small group, then it might be you. Here's a tip: you don't have to answer every question and comment on every point. Try to find a balance between the two extremes.

Be Consistent

Healthy relationships take time to grow. Quality time is great, but a great quantity of time is probably better. Commit with your group to show up every week (or whenever your group plans to meet), even when you don't feel like it. With only six sessions per book, if you miss just two meetings you'll have missed a third of what's presented in these pages. When you make a commitment to your small group a high priority, you're sure to build meaningful relationships.

Practice Honesty and Confidentiality

Strong relationships are only as solid as the trust they are built upon. Although it may be difficult, take a risk and be honest with your answers. God wants you to be known by others! Then respect the risks others are taking and offer them the same love, grace, and forgiveness God does. Make confidentiality a nonnegotiable value for your small group. Nothing kills community like gossip.

Arrive Ready to Grow

You can always arrive prepared by praying ahead of time. Ask God to give you the courage to be honest and the discipline to respect others.

You aren't required to do any preparation in the book before you arrive (unless you're the leader—see page 86). If your leader chooses to, she may ask you to do the Disciple-

Doug Fields & Brett Eastman

Doug and Brett were part of the same small group for several years. Brett was the pastor of small groups at Saddleback Church where Doug is the pastor to students. Brett and a team of friends wrote DOING LIFETOGETHER, a group study for adults. Everyone loved it so much that they asked Doug to take the same theme and Bible verses and revise the other material for students. So even though Brett and Doug both had a hand in writing this book, the book you're using is written by Doug—and as a youth pastor, he's cheering you on in your small group experience. For more information on Doug and Brett, see page 152.

ship (GROWING) section ahead of time so that you'll have more time to discuss the other sections and make better use of your time.

Congratulations…

…for making a commitment to go through this material with your small group! Life change is within reach when people are united through the same commitment. Your participation in a small group can have a lasting and powerful impact on your life. Our prayer is that the questions and activities in this book help you grow closer to the other group member, and more importantly, to God.

If you're a small group leader to, please turn to page 87 for a brief instruction on how best to use this material.

SMALL GROUP COVENANT

One of the signs of a healthy small group is that all members understand its purpose. We've learned that members of good small groups make a bond, a commitment, or a covenant to one another.

Read through the following covenant as a group. Be sure to discuss your concerns and questions before you begin your first session. Please feel free to modify the covenant based on the needs and concerns of your particular group. Once you agree with the terms and are willing to commit to the covenant (as you've revised it), sign your own book and have the others sign yours.

With a covenant, your entire group will have the same purpose for your time together, allowing you to grow together and go deeper into your study of God's Word. Without a covenant, groups often find themselves meeting simply for the sake of meeting.

If your group decides to add some additional values, write them at the bottom of the covenant page. Your group may also want to create some rules (such as not interrupting when someone else is speaking or sitting up instead of lying down). You can list those at the bottom of the covenant page also.

Reviewing your group's covenant, values, and rules before each meeting can become a significant part of your small group experience.

A covenant is a binding agreement or contract. God made covenants with Noah, Abraham, and David, among others. Jesus is the fulfillment of a new covenant between God and his people.

SMALL GROUP COVENANT

I, _____, as a member of our small group, acknowledge my need for meaningful relationships with other believers. I agree that this small group community exists to help me deepen my relationships with God, Christians, and other people in my life. I commit to the following:

Consistency

I will give my best effort to attend each of our group meetings.

Honesty

I will take risks to share truthfully about the personal issues in my life.

Confidentiality

I will support the foundation of trust in our small group by not participating in gossip. I will not reveal personal information shared by others during our meetings.

Respect

I will help create a safe environment for our small group members by listening carefully and not making fun of others.

Prayer

I commit to pray regularly for the people in our small group.

Accountability

I will allow the people in my small group to hold me accountable for growing spiritually and living a life that honors God.

This covenant, signed by all the members in this group, reflects our commitment to one another.

Date:

Names:

Additional values our small group members agree to

Additional rules our small group members agree to

AS I HAVE LOVED YOU

 LEADERS, READ PAGE 86.

Courtney was sick most of the year, missed a lot of school, and was diagnosed with leukemia in June. While she should have been out celebrating summer freedom, instead she stayed at home, away from people. She didn't want any visitors because of how chemotherapy made her look and feel—her treatments left her bald and bloated, and she felt ugly. While Courtney knew she needed the treatments to stay alive, she was still concerned and embarrassed by her appearance.

By the end of the summer, Courtney's chemo was over, and her doctors assured her that she was in remission. This answer to prayer meant that Courtney could return to school as soon as she regained her energy!

Only a few of her closest friends kept up with Courtney's progress over the summer. Most students didn't even know the extent of her illness. As the first day of school neared, she became painfully nervous when she thought about walking across campus without any hair. At one point she cried out in frustration, "I'd rather die than go to school bald!"

Courtney's mom was in a Bible study with several women who had daughters Courtney's age. As the start of the new school year approached, some of the families from Bible study began to talk about how they might help Courtney feel good about coming back to school. One girl, Sarah, mentioned an organization called "The Great Shave" that raised money for leukemia patients. Sarah talked three of her friends into the cutting their hair (and ultimately shaving their heads) in honor of Courtney and her battle with leukemia. Their cut hair would then be used to make a wig that Courtney could wear until her own hair grew back.

These friends expressed a great love and sacrifice by starting the school year bald! Word about this sacrificial act and the reasons behind it spread throughout the campus, and Courtney and her friends became heroes.

Expressing love often comes with a cost. Courtney's friends were willing to sacrifice their own appearances to show her love. Your friendships may never require a sacrifice like theirs, but as you consider Jesus' words about love in this session, ask yourself, "How much am I willing to sacrifice for a friend?"

♥ FELLOWSHIP: CONNECTING YOUR HEART TO OTHERS

Goal: To share about your life and listen attentively to others, caring about what they share

Just a reminder: There probably isn't enough time in your small-group session to answer every question. Instead choose which ones you'll answer, and then answer the others on your own time. Have fun!

Because you're learning in a small group setting, you're not learning alone. You may already have formed impressions of the other people in your group without knowing much about them. This fellowship section (which is in all six sessions) will provide an opportunity for your group's members to get to know each other better. When you open up a little bit of your life and share pieces of your story, you'll get to know each other better.

Just as the stories of Jesus will give you a clearer picture of him, others' stories will give you a clearer picture of who they really are. To get the most out of this group, it's worth taking a risk, revealing some of yourself and carefully listening to others' hearts. While it can seem scary at first, it does get easier to open up. The benefits of getting to know each other in this way are huge. Be sure to have someone keep an eye on your time in this section, or you may spend your entire time here and not get any further!

Just a reminder: there probably isn't enough time in your small group session to answer every question. Instead choose which ones you'll answer, and then answer the others on your own time. Have fun!

1. Take turns giving your short responses to these questions:

   - Name a food you love…
   - Name a TV show you love…
   - Name an experience you loved…
   - Name a person you love…
   - Name one person you know loves you…

2. What's your first memory of experiencing God's love? (If you're new to this and haven't had an experience of God's love yet, don't worry—you're probably not the only one.)

If your group hasn't discussed the small group covenant on page 18, please take some time now to go through it. Make commitments to each other that your group time will reflect those values (and any additional ones you add). One sign of a healthy small group is that it begins each session by reading the covenant together as a constant reminder of what the group has committed to.

If your group hasn't discussed the small group covenant on page 18, please take some time now to go through it. Make commitments to each other that your group time will reflect those values (and any additional ones you add). One sign of a healthy small group is that it begins each session by reading the covenant together as a constant reminder of what the group has committed to.

DISCIPLESHIP: GROWING TO BE LIKE JESUS

Goal: To explore God's Word, gain biblical knowledge, and make personal applications

The true meaning of love is often diluted in our world—I "love" a slice of pizza and "love" my best friend. Even though we know we can't love food like people, the word *love* sure gets tossed around carelessly sometimes. Even when we take a moment to look at the most serious kind of love, it can be hard to understand fully. If you were to ask 10 people what true love is, you might get 10 different answers.

Jesus lived a life of perfect love, showing us the example of love we ought to follow. In this section, we're going to take a look at his model so that we can learn to love others more like Jesus.

Read John 15:9-17. (**If you don't have a Bible, the passage is on page 91.**)

1. Why do you think Jesus talks about the love of the Father?

2. According to this passage, what does it mean to remain in Jesus' love?

3. Based on your personal experience, what does it mean for you to remain in Jesus' love? Try to be specific!

4. Why is there a connection between obedience and remaining in Jesus' love?

5. Why is this particular teaching important? Why did Jesus tell us to remain in his love? (You may need to reread the Bible passage to answer this question.)

6. As the Father loves Jesus, he loves us. We're to remain in Jesus' love by obeying his commands so we may have joy. Would anyone who knows you describe your life as joyful?

7. If so, how does joy impact your life? If not, what do you think is keeping you from joy?

8. Jesus tells us to obey his commands. What is his command in this passage?

9. What is the ultimate expression of love (verse 13)? On a practical level, what might this look like for you?

10. In your opinion, why is it sometimes difficult to love others? What has kept you from loving others the way you should?

11. What is the significance of being Jesus' friend as opposed to his servant? (You may need to reread the passage to see how the text answers this question.)

12. In verse 16, Jesus talks about the idea of being chosen first. Why is this important? What does this have to do with love and loving others?

13. Let's get personal: how well do you love others like Jesus demonstrated? What is something practical you can do next week to show love? (As a group, write these things down so you can pray for each other and "check in" with each other the next time you meet.)

⌁ EVANGELISM: SHARING YOUR STORY AND GOD'S STORY

Goal: To consider how the truths from this session might be applied to your relationships with unbelievers

Many small groups have such a good time together that they don't want to open up to new people. It's easy to think, "Why start over with strangers when we've already begun to develop a good group?" It's a fair question, and you may find that your leaders want to keep your small group closed for now. But for the sake of this discussion about love, think about some non-Christian friends to whom you can show Jesus' love in stronger ways.

1. Think about the following three areas of your life. Write down the names of non-Christians you know in each of the three circles (or use initials if you don't want to go public with their names).

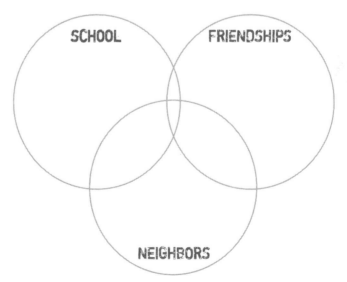

SCHOOL

FRIENDSHIPS

NEIGHBORS

2. Which of these friends can you imagine yourself inviting to a church event? If your group isn't the right place to invite your friends, what is an appropriate place?

MINISTRY: SERVING OTHERS IN LOVE

Goal: To recognize and take advantage of opportunities to serve others

1. How can you show the love of Jesus to those people you noted in the previous section? Write your ideas next to their names.

2. How do acts of love connect to the goal of ministry?

WORSHIP: SURRENDERING YOUR LIFE TO HONOR GOD

Goal: To focus on God's presence

When you clearly see Jesus as the One who laid down his life for you, worship is a natural response to his act of sacrificial love.

1. Take some time to respond to Jesus' love for you. Worship him through reading the Bible and prayer. Read Psalm 139 aloud together. (See page 91 if you don't have your Bible.) This Psalm contains a repeated phrase that makes it ideal for reading aloud. Have one person read the first line of each verse ("Give thanks to the LORD, for he is good"), and let the whole group repeat the following verse ("His love endures forever").

For the health of your small group, be sure to read the clique section on pages 111-112. It's vital for your group to decide at this first session whether you can invite friends to join your group. Talk about the structure of your group and stick to your decision. If you decide the answer is no, you may be able to invite friends to join you in the next EXPERIENCING CHRIST TOGETHER book—there are six of them, so there's plenty of time! If you're a small-group leader, see the Small Group Leader Checklist on page 86.

2. Share at least one way the group can pray for you this week. You can record prayer requests starting on page 144.

3. As you listen to your group members' prayer requests, think about how you might show love to each of them throughout the week.

You'll find three prayer resources in the appendices in the back of this book. By reading them (and possibly discussing them), you'll find your group prayer time more rewarding.
• Praying in Your Small Group (pages 138-139). Read this article on your own before the next session.
• Prayer Request Guidelines (pages 140-141). Read and discuss these guidelines as a group.
• Prayer Options (pages 142-143). Refer to this list for ideas to add variety to your prayer time.

AT HOME THIS WEEK

One of the consistent values of our LIFETOGETHER books is that we want you to have options for growing spiritually on your own during the week. To help with this "on your own" value, we'll give you five options. If you do these, you'll have more to contribute when you return to your small group, and you'll begin to develop spiritual habits that can last your entire life. Here are the five you'll see after every section. (You might try to do one per day on the days after your small group meets.)

Option 1: A Weekly Reflection

After each session you'll find a quick, one-page self-evaluation that reflects the five areas of your spiritual life found in this book (fellowship, discipleship, ministry, evangelism, and worship). After each evaluation, you decide if there's anything you'll do differently with your life. This page is all for *you*. It's not intended as a report card that you turn into your small group leader. The first evaluation is on page 29.

Option 2: Daily Bible Readings

On pages 122-123 you'll find a list of Bible passages that will help you read through an entire section of the Bible in 30 days. If you choose this option, try to read one of the assigned passages each day. Highlight key verses in your Bible, reflect on them, journal about them, or write down any questions you have from your reading. We want to encourage you to take time to read God's love letter—the Bible. You'll find helpful tips in "How to Study the Bible on Your Own" (pages 124-126).

Option 3: Memory Verses

"I HAVE HIDDEN YOUR WORD IN MY HEART THAT I MIGHT NOT SIN AGAINST YOU." (PSALM 119:11)

Option 4: Journaling

You'll find blank pages for journaling beginning on page 132. At the end of each session, you'll find questions to get your thoughts going—but you aren't limited to answering the questions listed. Use these pages to reflect, write a letter to God, note what you're learning, compose prayer, ask questions, draw pictures, record your thoughts, or take notes if your small group is using the EXPERIENCING CHRIST TOGETHER DVD teachings. For some suggestions about journaling, turn to "Journaling: Snapshots of Your Heart" on pages 129-131.

For this session, choose one or more questions to kick-start your journaling.

- I'm excited to be in a group because…
- If someone asked me to describe Jesus, I would say…
- Jesus would want me to know…

Option 5: Wrap It Up

Go back through the session and answer the questions your group didn't have time to discuss.

LEARN A LITTLE MORE

Goal: To help you better understand the Scripture passage you studied in this session by highlighting key words and other important information.

Of the five options listed here, mark the option(s) that seem most appealing to you. Share with your group the one(s) you plan to do in the upcoming week. This helps you keep one another accountable as you continue to study and grow on your own.

Remain in my love (John 15:9)

Jesus uses the word *remain* (or *abide*) seven times in John 15:1-10. The word means to last a long time, to endure, or to stay. When you consider that definition in light of Jesus' love, it's an awesome thought. Jesus' love endures—in fact, it lasts forever. Jesus' love withstands the test of time and trouble. To remain in Jesus is to stay with him, go where he goes, and maintain constant awareness of his presence and his love—and therefore to love as Jesus loves.

Love (15:12)

The Greek word for *love* in this passage is *agape*. *Agape* love is used to speak of the love of God or unconditional love—the kind of love that expects nothing in return.

Lay down his life for his friends (15:13)

Jesus has a radical definition for love: it requires the ultimate sacrifice—your very life! Jesus spoke these words to his disciples the night before he gave up his life for the sins of the world. (It's important to note that God never requires anything of us that he didn't first require of Jesus.)

You did not choose me, but I chose you (John 15:16)

This passage is all about love, and what love really is. Love begins with the love of God the Father to Jesus the Son, and from Jesus to the world. It's important to remember that God loved us long before we loved him. This truth should lead to an attitude of humility and serves as our example for loving others. We must not wait until we are loved first before we love others. Just as Jesus loved us first, so should we love others first and not wait for them to love us.

FOR DEEPER STUDY ON YOUR OWN

1. For a broader context of this passage, read John 15-17.

2. Read 1 John 4:7-21. Why does John say love is so important for us to practice?

3. Read Romans 5:6-8. The Apostle Paul emphasizes that Jesus' love was unusual. If it is so unusual, can we still expect to follow his example?

A WEEKLY REFLECTION

Take a minute to reflect on how well you've been doing in the following five areas of your spiritual life this week—a 10 means you did an amazing job. This reflection can serve as a spiritual gauge to help you consider some very important areas. This is for your personal evaluation and growth; it's NOT a test—no one else needs to see it.

FELLOWSHIP: CONNECTING YOUR HEART TO OTHERS

How well did I connect with other Christians?

1   2   3   4   5   6   7   8   9   10

DISCIPLESHIP: GROWING TO BE LIKE JESUS

How well did I take steps to grow spiritually and deepen my faith on my own?

1   2   3   4   5   6   7   8   9   10

MINISTRY: SERVING OTHERS IN LOVE

How well did I recognize opportunities to serve others and follow through?

1   2   3   4   5   6   7   8   9   10

EVANGELISM: SHARING YOUR STORY AND GOD'S STORY

How well did I engage in spiritual conversations with non-Christians?

1   2   3   4   5   6   7   8   9   10

WORSHIP: SURRENDERING YOUR LIFE TO HONOR GOD

How well did I focus on God's presence and honor him with my life? Was my relationship with God a primary focus?

1   2   3   4   5   6   7   8   9   10

When you finish, celebrate the areas where you feel good and consider how you can use those strengths to help others in their journey to be more like Jesus. You might also want to take time to identify some potential areas for growth.

LOVE THAT SHOWS UP

 LEADERS, READ PAGE 86.

Kelly was a high-school senior and captain of her cheerleading squad. She did all the fun stunts and flew high when her squad mates tossed her in the air. Then one afternoon at practice Kelly's teammates didn't catch her—and she hit the ground hard and broke her leg and hip. She was unable to attend school for the remaining six weeks of the year. Not only would she miss finals, but also her senior prom. Prior to the accident, Kelly heard rumors that Matt was going to ask her to prom. Matt and Kelly had been friends for a long time—they went to church together—but recently she'd started to think of him in a boyfriend-type way.

The weeks of healing were painful. It wasn't just her leg that hurt; it was emotionally hard not being around friends, school, and church. But Kelly trusted God and knew he would create something good from this situation.

Kelly's small group knew she was hurting and not only prayed diligently but also made sacrifices to help her through this difficult time. They made sure Kelly got notes from her classes and kept her updated on all school events.

Kelly never asked her friends to do any of this—they simply anticipated her needs and took action. As a result, Kelly felt secure and confident as finals approached despite her sadness about missing prom with Matt.

On prom night, Kelly's girlfriends from her small group came over dressed for prom. They brought Kelly flowers and a crown and announced her Prom Queen for the evening—and not one of them left her side the entire night. They laughed, told stories, and did silly dances.

Kelly was so thankful that her friends gave up such an important night for her—and for the many other generous acts throughout her recovery. She had never before experienced the power of genuine community until these generous acts were done on her behalf.

In this session you'll think about what it might mean for you to care for others in generous ways…just like Kelly's friends did for her.

❤ FELLOWSHIP: CONNECTING YOUR HEART TO OTHERS

Goal: To share about your life and listen attentively to others, caring about what they share

Since you'll be talking about how to graciously care for others, begin your group time by sharing the most outrageous act of caring you've witnessed. For example, maybe a parent or a relative or a Christian friend cared for someone in such a way that it left an impression you'll never forget.

DISCIPLESHIP: GROWING TO BE LIKE JESUS

Goal: To explore God's Word, gain biblical knowledge, and make personal applications

The story of Jesus raising Lazarus from the dead is a model of sacrificial love. It's important to note that Lazarus, Martha, and Mary were some of Jesus' best friends (see Luke 10:38-42). Because of this, Jesus' disciples weren't surprised when Jesus wanted to go to the women when Lazarus got sick. But as you'll see, Jesus' visit wasn't just an inconvenience in his busy schedule. His visit placed his life at risk. His disciples were blown away that Jesus was willing to express this kind of love for his friends. To them this was extreme love, and it really expanded their limited ideas of what love is.

Read John 11:1-44. **(If you don't have a Bible, the passage is on pages 93-95.)**

As a group, outline the main points in this passage. Once everyone has a handle on the story's "big picture," study the details of each of the following sections or pick one of the three to study in depth (based on your time).

Read John 11:1-16.

1. What does this passage tell us about the relationship between Jesus and Lazarus, Mary, and Martha?

2. Why do you think Jesus didn't leave as soon as he heard Lazarus was sick?

3. Why was Jesus "glad" (11:15) he didn't keep Lazarus from dying?

4. What is Thomas typically remembered for? (See John 20:20-27.) How does this passage present a different picture of Thomas?

Read John 11:17-37.

5. Three times this passage mentions Jesus could have kept Lazarus from death (verses 21, 32, 37). Why do you think the author of this Gospel points this out?

6. It's clear that Martha had a strong faith in Jesus. What is it she believed about him?

7. Why did Jesus claim to be the resurrection and the life? Didn't Martha already believe this about Jesus?

8. How did Jesus expand their belief about the resurrection?

9. Why did Jesus cry if he knew Lazarus was about to rise from the dead—an act that would bring glory to God and increase the faith of his followers? Did Jesus really "miss" Lazarus when he knew he was about to see him?

Read John 11:38-44.

10. Why did Jesus pray before he called out to Lazarus?

11. It's clear that Martha believed in the power of the resurrection to come, but God's plan was to demonstrate his power in the present. Do you ever find yourself trusting God to take care of the future but not relying on him for the present moment?

12. What would your life look like if you truly believed God's power was available right now and every moment in your life? How would it be different?

MINISTRY: SERVING OTHERS IN LOVE

Goal: To recognize and take advantage of opportunities to serve others

I want to encourage your group to do something significant for other people in your church for no apparent reason other than to practice showing up and caring. You might show up to an elderly person's house and mow his lawn or a widow's house and rake her leaves and wash her car…just because.

1. Think of one person in your church whom your group could surprise with an act of caring. What could you do for that person? Now make sure you set a date to do it before the end of this session.

2. If your group can't decide on an action, what about you individually? Can you make something happen by yourself? If so, record your idea.

EVANGELISM: SHARING YOUR STORY AND GOD'S STORY

Goal: To consider how the truths from this session might be applied to your relationships with unbelievers

1. In the previous section, the idea was to care for someone in the church. What do you think it might communicate if you did this for someone outside the church? What's the connection between helping people and sharing the gospel with them?

2. How can you communicate and reflect the love of Jesus without being perceived as obnoxious? Be as specific as possible.

🚶 WORSHIP: SURRENDERING YOUR LIFE TO HONOR GOD

Goal: To focus on God's presence

Jesus was constantly faithful to God. When he learned of Lazarus' illness, rather than dropping everything and going to Bethany, he "delayed" the trip to continue his work. When his disciples tried to warn him against going, he could not be persuaded—he was obedient to God and loving to his friends.

1. Sometimes God's calling on our lives seems contrary to good judgment. Share about a time when you needed to rely on God's timing and plans rather than your own.

2. Here's a sample prayer to help you begin the process of developing a heart of compassion.

GOD, PLEASE HELP MY HEART TO BREAK OVER THE HURTS OF OTHERS. I WANT TO SEE HURT THE WAY YOU DO, AND I WANT TO BE MORE TENDER TO FEEL PAIN LIKE YOU MUST FEEL PAIN. I CAN'T DO THIS ON MY OWN. I NEED YOUR HELP! AMEN.

3. If you have time, write a similar prayer below that is more specific to your own life. If you feel comfortable, share your prayer with your group.

4. End your time by praying together.

AT HOME THIS WEEK

Option 1: A Weekly Reflection

Take another self-evaluation that reflects five areas of your spiritual life (fellowship, discipleship, ministry, evangelism, and worship). See page 38.

Option 2: Daily Bible Readings

Check out the Bible reading plan on pages 122-123.

Option 3: Memory Verses

Memorize another verse from pages 127-128.

Option 4: Journaling

Choose one or more of the following options:

- Write down whatever is on your mind.
- Read your journal entry from last week and write a reflection about it.
- Respond to these questions: Where have I missed an opportunity to show love to someone, up close? Why did I pass on that opportunity?

Option 5: Wrap It Up

Write out your answers to any questions that you didn't answer during your small group time.

LEARN A LITTLE MORE

Bethany (John 11:1)

Bethany is a village about two miles from Jerusalem on the Mount of Olives. It was located near the road between Jerusalem and Jericho. Jesus would visit Bethany again just before the Passover (John 12:1).

A man who walks by day will not stumble (11:9)

Jesus didn't live according to human wisdom; his plans were an expression of his faithfulness to God. Those who live according to God's way walk in the day and do not stumble. In essence, Jesus meant, "We're doing the right thing; nothing can slow us down."

I am the resurrection (11:25)

Jewish groups had different ideas and expectations about life after death. Some believed life ended at death. Others believed that souls were everlasting and would be liberated at death. Jesus was among those Jews who believed God was going to resurrect his people whole—soul and body—when it was time for God's kingdom. And Jesus went even further: He claimed that the resurrection was possible only through him.

Deeply moved in spirit and troubled (11:33)

The words used here don't mean Jesus was sad over the loss of Lazarus—after all, Jesus knew Lazarus would be alive again in minutes. Rather, the words refer to anger. Jesus was angry at death and its negative effect on Mary, Martha, and their community.

FOR DEEPER STUDY ON YOUR OWN

1   Learn more about Mary and Martha. Check out Luke 10:38-42 and John 12:1-8.

2. See how Timothy and Epaphroditus cared for Paul in prison (Philippians 2:19-30). Why did Epaphroditus risk his health for Paul's sake? Where do friends draw the line when it comes to caring?

A WEEKLY REFLECTION

Take a minute to reflect on how well you've been doing in the following five areas of your spiritual life this week—a 10 means you did an amazing job. This reflection can serve as a spiritual gauge to help you consider some very important areas. This is for your personal evaluation and growth; it's NOT a test—no one else needs to see it.

FELLOWSHIP: CONNECTING YOUR HEART TO OTHERS

How well did I connect with other Christians?

1   2   3   4   5   6   7   8   9   10

DISCIPLESHIP: GROWING TO BE LIKE JESUS

How well did I take steps to grow spiritually and deepen my faith on my own?

1   2   3   4   5   6   7   8   9   10

MINISTRY: SERVING OTHERS IN LOVE

How well did I recognize opportunities to serve others and follow through?

1   2   3   4   5   6   7   8   9   10

EVANGELISM: SHARING YOUR STORY AND GOD'S STORY

How well did I engage in spiritual conversations with non-Christians?

1   2   3   4   5   6   7   8   9   10

WORSHIP: SURRENDERING YOUR LIFE TO HONOR GOD

How well did I focus on God's presence and honor him with my life? Was my relationship with God a primary focus?

1   2   3   4   5   6   7   8   9   10

When you finish, celebrate the areas where you feel good and consider how you can use those strengths to help others in their journey to be more like Jesus. You might also want to take time to identify some potential areas for growth.

SESSION 3
LOVING DIFFICULT PEOPLE

 LEADERS, READ PAGE 86.

Buddy and Cole met the first week of their freshman year of high school. Buddy was quiet and insecure. Cole noticed and began to include Buddy in his group of friends. At first their friendship focused on gaining popularity, acting cool, and experimenting with partying and drinking. But as Cole began to learn more about Jesus, his love, and his ways, he lost interest in the party scene. He was growing spiritually and saw how empty his popularity search was. But Buddy kept searching for popularity—and slowly they drifted apart.

A couple of years later, Cole reconnected with Buddy and discovered that Buddy's life was a mess. He drank heavily, smoked pot, and admitted that he was addicted to pornography. Because of Cole's relationship with Jesus, he knew he couldn't leave Buddy alone in his addictions. He jumped back into Buddy's life and encouraged him to get help. Buddy agreed but continued giving in to his same struggles. Cole was consistent in his friendship and didn't leave him alone—slowly he got through to him. Cole carefully explained to Buddy why he had a relationship with Jesus and how he felt God's presence through his ups and downs.

Buddy wanted what Cole had and eventually began to make changes, but he would often tell Cole how he sometimes returned to addictive ways even when he didn't want to. Patiently, Cole continued to care for his friend and acted as an accountability partner to help keep him from returning to his former lifestyle.

Today Buddy is free from his addictive behaviors and growing stronger in Jesus. It was Cole's commitment to be with Buddy—despite his addictions—that helped Buddy find hope and healing in Jesus. Cole was a great example of what it means for a follower of Jesus to hang in there with friends who are struggling.

It's easy to show love to people who are easy to love. But it's difficult to express love and friendship to those who have consistent problems or obvious sins in their lives. Cole fought through this difficulty and modeled the love of Jesus for Buddy's sake. That's what this session is about—learning to love difficult people.

♥ FELLOWSHIP: CONNECTING YOUR HEART TO OTHERS'

Goal: To share about your life and listen attentively to others, caring about what they share

1. On a scale of 1 to 10, how has your week been? In less than a minute, pick a number and explain your answer.

1   2   3   4   5   6   7   8   9   10

Terrible… I'd rather be kicked in the head… Okay… Better than most weeks… GREAT!

2. Name something another person does that really ticks you off (littering, cussing, not listening, being obnoxious, and so on). Don't say *who* does it—just share what it is that drives you crazy. Why do you think it bothers you so much? **Slow drivers**

DISCIPLESHIP: GROWING TO BE LIKE JESUS

Goal: To explore God's Word, gain biblical knowledge, and make personal applications

The passage you're about to discuss is really amazing! It's about a woman caught in the act of adultery and brought to Jesus for judgment. Jesus blew the crowd away by releasing this lawfully condemned sinner. Jesus did something most other religious leaders of his day rarely did—he gave a sinner a second chance. No one else taught or modeled this kind of love that transforms hearts and builds relationships—the kind of love directed toward those who are difficult to love.

Read John 8:1-11. (If you don't have a Bible, the passage is on page 95.)

1. Why were the Pharisees trying to trap Jesus?

2. Where was the man who committed adultery? What do you think happened to him?

3. Why do you think Jesus wrote on the ground? What do you think he wrote?

4. Take a look at Jesus' answer to the Pharisees (verse 7). What did he mean? Why is that important?

5. Jesus said, "Do not think that I have come to abolish the Law or the Prophets; I have not come to abolish them but to fulfill them" (Matthew 5:17). Doesn't it seem as though Jesus' response to this woman contradicts the Law of Moses? Why, or why not?

6. Why do you think Jesus forgave the woman? Are there any key words or phrases in the verses that help answer this question?

7. If the central teaching in this passage is about forgiveness, are Christians allowed to do whatever they want since Jesus will always forgive us? Explain your answer.

8. Why do you think forgiveness is so powerful in relationships?

B+

9. On a letter-grade scale of A to F, how would you rate yourself as a forgiving person? Explain your grade.

10. Name a time you received forgiveness from another person. How did it make you feel?

11. What happens to people who don't forgive others? What do their relationships look like?

12. Is there someone who has hurt or offended you whom you need to forgive? Who is that person? How can you make things right this week?

MINISTRY: SERVING OTHERS IN LOVE

Goal: To recognize and take advantage of opportunities to serve others

As I write this, I'm thinking of a mom who's going through a difficult time with her daughter. The mom is trying her best, but her daughter is hard to love right now. Every time I see the mom, she's discouraged—but her faith in Jesus gives her hope that her daughter will change.

1. Without going into specifics about the person, do you know someone like the daughter? What makes this person so difficult to love?

2. How does judging others affect the way you love and serve them?

3. Turn to page 101 and write an uplifting letter to encourage and minister to someone you know who is discouraged. Then either tear the page from the book and give it/mail it to the person, or rewrite the letter in another format and send it. A small note of encouragement like this can make a big difference for the person who receives it.

EVANGELISM: SHARING YOUR STORY AND GOD'S STORY

Goal: To consider how the truths from this session might be applied to your relationships with unbelievers

1. If you haven't already, think of a person you find difficult to love. (Don't share the name of the person with your group.) How can you care for this person in a manner that would honor God and express his love?

2. Have one person in the group share her situation and use it to come up with a model for how to express love to someone who's difficult to love. Write down the specific action steps you could take to show love to this person. List the steps below.

3. Now go back and tailor these steps to fit your own situation. *1, Say It, repent*
7. give, forgive.
3, pray for them

⚊ WORSHIP: SURRENDERING YOUR LIFE TO HONOR GOD

Goal: To focus on God's presence

Surrendering your heart to God isn't easy. When we don't surrender our hearts to God on a regular basis, we can become difficult to love. Surrendering is a necessary, continual action in the life of a growing follower of Jesus. This action can become easier when you develop the habit of taking difficult areas of your life—sin, temptation, disappointment, anxiety, sadness, anger, etc.—before God and admitting that you need help. Then after you've gone to God in private, it can be powerful to share those same struggles with others in your small-group community. Your group can then become part of the helping and healing process. Once you admit these difficult areas, they're no longer secret. And with the help of God and others, sin doesn't have to have power over you.

1. At this moment, are there areas in your life that you wish you could share but find it too difficult right now? (If so, that's okay.)

2. This session has been about loving people who are difficult to love. Before ending your group's time together, consider those things that can make you difficult to love. Can you think of anything? What is it?

3. Consider praying this prayer silently before your group closes in prayer:

   God, I need help with _____ (what you wrote in response to question 2). Please give me the courage to share it with others and the wisdom to learn how to get help.

4. Close your time in prayer.

AT HOME THIS WEEK

Option 1: A Weekly Reflection

Take another self-evaluation that reflects five areas of your spiritual life (fellowship, discipleship, ministry, evangelism, and worship). See page 49.

Option 2: Daily Bible Readings

Check out the Bible reading plan on pages 122-123.

Option 3: Memory Verses

Memorize another verse from pages 127-128.

Option 4: Journaling

Choose one or more of the following options:

- Write down whatever is on your mind.
- Read your journal entry from last week and write a reflection about it.
- Respond to these questions: How am I like Cole in the story on page 41? How am I like Buddy? Where do I need the most help in my life? What scares me about asking my small group for help?

Option 5: Wrap It Up

Write out your answers to any questions that you didn't answer during your small group time.

LEARN A LITTLE MORE

Mount of Olives (John 8:1)

The Mount of Olives is a small ridge of three summits just east of Jerusalem.

Moses' Law (8:5)

See Leviticus 20:10 and Deuteronomy 22:22. The Law of Moses says that both the man and woman caught in adultery were to be condemned (judged guilty). The man is absent in this passage, but it is clear that the religious leaders were more interested in trapping Jesus than being faithful to the Law of Moses.

They were using this question as a trap, in order to have a basis for accusing him (8:6)

The religious leaders thought they had Jesus in an inescapable trap. If Jesus said, "Yes, condemn the woman to death," he would have upheld the Law of Moses, but he would have been guilty before Rome, which ruled over the Jewish people and allowed them to govern themselves in very limited ways. One of the areas Jews couldn't oversee was the death penalty—that could only be carried out by Rome. On the other hand, if Jesus had said, "No, do not condemn her," he would have been in direct contradiction to the Law of Moses. He would have lost either way.

FOR DEEPER STUDY ON YOUR OWN

Check out other teachings from Jesus about forgiveness in Matthew 18:21-35 and Luke 6:27-34. What do you learn from these passages?

A WEEKLY REFLECTION

Take a minute to reflect on how well you've been doing in the following five areas of your spiritual life this week—a 10 means you did an amazing job. This reflection can serve as a spiritual gauge to help you consider some very important areas. This is for your personal evaluation and growth; it's NOT a test—no one else needs to see it.

FELLOWSHIP: CONNECTING YOUR HEART TO OTHERS

How well did I connect with other Christians?

1   2   3   4   5   6   7   8   9   10

DISCIPLESHIP: GROWING TO BE LIKE JESUS

How well did I take steps to grow spiritually and deepen my faith on my own?

1   2   3   4   5   6   7   8   9   10

MINISTRY: SERVING OTHERS IN LOVE

How well did I recognize opportunities to serve others and follow through?

1   2   3   4   5   6   7   8   9   10

EVANGELISM: SHARING YOUR STORY AND GOD'S STORY

How well did I engage in spiritual conversations with non-Christians?

1   2   3   4   5   6   7   8   9   10

WORSHIP: SURRENDERING YOUR LIFE TO HONOR GOD

How well did I focus on God's presence and honor him with my life? Was my relationship with God a primary focus?

1   2   3   4   5   6   7   8   9   10

When you finish, celebrate the areas where you feel good and consider how you can use those strengths to help others in their journey to be more like Jesus. You might also want to take time to identify some potential areas for growth.

TRUTHFUL BUT TENDER

 LEADERS, READ PAGE 86.

Things seemed to come easily for Molly—grades, friends, money. She was attractive, drove a nice car, and was typically the life of a party. But while Molly appeared to have it all together on the outside, she had a difficult time making good decisions. She was impulsive, indecisive, and intensely insecure. It seemed as though every time her small group met, the prayer time was dedicated to Molly and her problem of the day.

One time she parked in a handicapped space because she only needed to stop in a store "for a minute." She got a $200 parking ticket and never told her parents. Another time she forgot to show up to baby-sit for someone and didn't tell her parents that the family was disappointed in her flaky behavior. Recently she stole a pair of earrings to impress some guys she was hanging out with.

Molly admitted all of this to her small group. The other girls encouraged Molly to do the right things...but they couldn't be with her all the time to make sure she did the right things. They knew Molly had a difficult time accepting herself and suffered from poor self-esteem. To spare her feelings, they didn't confront her behavior—they didn't say anything because they didn't want her to feel judged or hurt.

Finally the group members decided Molly's game was getting old, and they had to confront her reckless decisions. They told Molly that she was hurting others, and that they couldn't continue to keep silent about it. But they also told her how much they cared for her and how they would gladly step deeper into her life and hold her more accountable for her decisions.

It was that confrontation that prompted Molly to change. She decided that since these girls cared so much about her, she would respond by taking an honest look at her life and behavior. Since then Molly's choices haven't been perfect, but she has taken more responsibility for herself, and her life is improving. Her small group talks about her growth and change at every meeting, and Molly feels like God has blessed her and the group because of the faith the girls in it showed by expressing honesty and love.

That's the challenge for this session—how to be truthful and tender at the same time. It's quite a challenge! But Jesus was the master, and in this session you will see him model it for us.

♥ FELLOWSHIP: CONNECTING YOUR HEART TO OTHERS

Goal: To share about your life and listen attentively to others, caring about what they share

In this session you'll explore the tension between telling others what you really think (your perception of the truth) and not hurting their feelings with that truth.

If I see someone doing something wrong, I'm usually…

a. silent. I don't want to get into a fight or hurt other people's feelings; I'm not too comfortable with conflict.

b. blunt. I feel obligated to share my perception of the truth, and I'll usually take the risk that I'll hurt someone's feelings.

c. _____ (fill in your answer).

DISCIPLESHIP: GROWING TO BE LIKE JESUS

Goal: To explore God's Word, gain biblical knowledge, and make personal applications

Most of us struggle with confrontation—maybe we avoid it at any cost or maybe we blast others with the "truth" in a reckless manner…or something in between. Although most of us would prefer not to confront others if we don't have to, both extremes can lead to serious relational problems. We all need to hear the truth, but it's best to be gentle when you tell people what they need to hear. In this passage, Jesus gives Peter a great compliment as well as a stern rebuke. Jesus always knew the perfect thing to say to help a person grow.

Read Matthew 16:13-28. **(If you don't have a Bible, the passage is on pages 95-96.)**

1. Why do you think Jesus asked his disciples about his reputation (verse 13)?

2. What was the significance of Peter's answer? What did it mean to call Jesus "the Christ, the Son of the living God"? to show that it has revealed to Peter

3. Why did Jesus bless Peter? What did his blessing mean?

4. Why didn't Jesus want the disciples to tell the world who he was?

5. Why did Jesus have to suffer "many things"? How does this relate to Jesus as Savior?

6. Why did Peter say Jesus didn't need to suffer?

7. Jesus called Peter "Satan" in verse 23. What do you think of Jesus' response to Peter? Was it too harsh? Why, or why not?

8. Divide this passage into two sections: verses 16-20 and verses 21-28. What are some of the connections you see between the two sections of Scripture?

9. Jesus excelled at teaching the truth. He never shied away from saying difficult things. In this passage, what is one teaching from Jesus that is difficult for you to deal with right now? Explain.

MINISTRY: SERVING OTHERS IN LOVE

Goal: To recognize and take advantage of opportunities to serve others

1. If your group is comfortable with each other, role-playing may be a good way to turn this lesson of tender truth-telling into a practical exercise. Try this and see if you can't get some experience with conflict in a thoughtful, God-honoring manner.

Take turns having one person in your group play the role of someone who always puts others down. Even though this person says "just kidding" and the comments should be taken in fun, others find them hurtful.

Have another person in your group confront this person with both truth and tenderness. This person should try to be truthful and kind, regardless of the other person's response. The person being confronted may become defensive—something many of us do when faced with something we'd rather not see about ourselves. Keep in mind Jesus' example and teaching—be honest, but don't get caught in anger or judgment.

The rest of the people in your group are observers trying to learn how to best confront in a caring way. Give the two volunteers a few minutes to play out their conversation. Then discuss together what worked well and what could be improved. Be both truthful and tender in evaluating each other—you'll all see that this isn't always easy to do!

☞ EVANGELISM: SHARING YOUR STORY AND GOD'S STORY

Goal: To consider how the truths from this session might be applied to your relationships with unbelievers

Part of developing an evangelistic mindset involves understanding how those who don't have a relationship with Jesus might view God, Jesus, church, Christians, and other ideas associated with Christianity.

1. Do you think the following statement is true or false? Explain your answer.

> "CHRISTIANS OUGHT TO CONFRONT
> NON-CHRISTIANS WITH THE TRUTH MORE
> OFTEN SO THEY CAN KNOW THE ERROR OF
> THEIR WAYS AND COME TO FAITH IN JESUS."

2. Do you think your confrontation style should be different when confronting a non-Christian? Why, or why not?

🚶 WORSHIP: SURRENDERING YOUR LIFE TO HONOR GOD

Goal: To focus on God's presence

1. Which of the following two prayers do you need to pray more often?

Patrick
1st

"GOD, HELP ME TO BE BRAVE SO I CAN SPEAK THE TRUTH."

Jay
2nd

"GOD, PLEASE HELP ME TO BE TENDER WHEN I SPEAK TO THIS PERSON."

2. Share your answer with your group and then pray for each other before you leave.

AT HOME THIS WEEK

Option 1: A Weekly Reflection

Take another self-evaluation that reflects five areas of your spiritual life (fellowship, discipleship, ministry, evangelism, and worship). See page 58.

Option 2: Daily Bible Readings

Check out the Bible reading plan on pages 122-123.

Option 3: Memory Verses

Memorize another verse from page 127.

Option 4: Journaling

Choose one or more of the following options:

- Write down whatever is on your mind.
- Read your journal entry from last week and write a reflection about it.
- Respond to these questions: What situation do I need to address with truth and tenderness? What am I going to say? (You may want to practice by writing down your initial words of confrontation.)

Option 5: Wrap It Up

Write out your answers to any questions that you didn't answer during your small group time.

LEARN A LITTLE MORE

Caesarea Philippi (Matthew 16:13)

Also known as Panias, Caesarea Philippi was located in the very northern end of Israel, some 40 miles north of Galilee.

Son of Man (16:13)

This term was Jesus' favorite title for himself; he used it more than 80 times in the Gospels. This title is significant for the following reasons: (a) Not only was Jesus divine (the "Son of God"), but he was also human; (b) His nationality was Jewish, but he was also a representative of all humanity; (c) This term originated in the Old Testament, where it was used in reference to the promised Messiah (Psalm 80:17). Using this title was another way for Jesus to announce to the world that he was the Messiah.

Christ (16:16)

Christ is Greek for "anointed one" and is the equivalent of the Hebrew word *Messiah*. In the Old Testament, priests, kings, and prophets were anointed with oil (it was poured on their heads) as a symbol of God's blessing, selection, and authorization for a special purpose. Although many people were anointed, the Old Testament promised the coming of "the Anointed One"—the Messiah. During the time of Jesus, the Jews were waiting for God to send the Messiah to save them; unfortunately, many Jews held expectations that were far different from what God intended. When Jesus came on the scene, many of them didn't believe in him because of their misperceptions.

Elijah

Elijah was a prophet from the Old Testament who performed many wonders in the name of the Lord. He was taken up to heaven in a chariot of fire, and among the Jews it was believed that Elijah would someday return. Jesus affirmed this belief in Mark 9:12.

FOR DEEPER STUDY ON YOUR OWN

1. For details about the amazing life of Elijah, read 1 Kings 16-19, 21 and 2 Kings 1-2.

A WEEKLY REFLECTION

Take a minute to reflect on how well you've been doing in the following five areas of your spiritual life this week—a 10 means you did an amazing job. This reflection can serve as a spiritual gauge to help you consider some very important areas. This is for your personal evaluation and growth; it's NOT a test—no one else needs to see it.

FELLOWSHIP: CONNECTING YOUR HEART TO OTHERS'

How well did I connect with other Christians?

1   2   3   4   5   6   7   8   9   10

DISCIPLESHIP: GROWING TO BE LIKE JESUS

How well did I take steps to grow spiritually and deepen my faith on my own?

1   2   3   4   5   6   7   8   9   10

MINISTRY: SERVING OTHERS IN LOVE

How well did I recognize opportunities to serve others and follow through?

1   2   3   4   5   6   7   8   9   10

EVANGELISM: SHARING YOUR STORY AND GOD'S STORY

How well did I engage in spiritual conversations with non-Christians?

1   2   3   4   5   6   7   8   9   10

WORSHIP: SURRENDERING YOUR LIFE TO HONOR GOD

How well did I focus on God's presence and honor him with my life? Was my relationship with God a primary focus?

1   2   3   4   5   6   7   8   9   10

When you finish, celebrate the areas where you feel good and consider how you can use those strengths to help others in their journey to be more like Jesus. You might also want to take time to identify some potential areas for growth.

EXTREME FORGIVENESS

 LEADERS, READ PAGE 86.

It had been a tough year for Josh. Moving from his childhood hometown was hard enough, but Josh's dad was working so much that Josh rarely ever saw him. When his dad was home, it wasn't all that pleasant anyway—his parents were constantly fighting over seemingly dumb stuff.

His family situation left Josh feeling alone and abandoned. One evening Josh's dad came home exhausted. He and his mom went into the bedroom to talk. As Josh watched television, he heard his mom scream something, slam the door, and storm out of the house. This kind of reaction didn't faze Josh anymore—screaming and fighting were becoming pretty normal in their home.

What *did* faze Josh was when his dad walked into the room and said, "Josh, I don't know any other way to say it, so here goes—I'm leaving your mother. I'm in love with another woman, and I need some changes to feel better about my life." The words ripped Josh's heart. His dad continued, "Your mother and I don't love each other anymore, and we haven't been a real family for the past few years. I'm sorry, Josh. I don't know what else to say."

Josh had never felt so much hatred in his life. He raged inside. Josh wanted to hit his father to make him feel the pain he felt. He couldn't believe his dad was just going to walk away from their family for some other woman. This reality was more than Josh could handle.

Josh struggled over the next few months, trying to understand why his father would do this. He wrestled with God and doubted he could ever find a way to forgive his father. After church youth group, an adult leader pulled Josh aside to talk about his anger toward his dad. This leader challenged Josh to try something that seemed impossible—to love his dad with the same love Jesus had for him. At first, Josh flinched at the idea. But later he promised he'd pray that God would give him the power to love his father with the love of Jesus.

As part of the divorce proceedings, Josh was asked to appear in court with his parents. He hadn't seen his dad since that night he left. Josh prayed the whole way to court. When he entered the room and saw his father, Josh slowly walked over and gave him a hug. He felt his anger lift and experienced the sense of peace he'd been praying for. Josh didn't have any words to say, but he didn't need them anymore. Even though the divorce went through, Josh knew he had done the right thing and responded in a way that was Christ-like—to love and forgive like Jesus. There's still a long journey ahead for Josh and his dad, but Josh now has hope that his relationship with his dad can grow.

It's easy to read about forgiveness, but it's difficult to pull it off in real life. As you go through this session, challenge each other to make forgiveness real in your lives.

♥ FELLOWSHIP: CONNECTING YOUR HEART TO OTHERS'

Goal: To share about your life and listen attentively to others, caring about what they share

1. What is something you think would be impossible for you to forgive?

2. Would you rather forgive a friend or forgive a stranger? Explain your answer.

DISCIPLESHIP: GROWING TO BE LIKE JESUS

Goal: To explore God's Word, gain biblical knowledge, and make personal applications

Get ready for some open-heart surgery. This Scripture passage is one of Jesus' most famous—but be warned: it's challenging!

Read Luke 6:27-38. (If you don't have a Bible, the passage is on pages 96-97)

1. In this passage, Jesus clearly outlines the difference between the world's standard and God's standard. Why do you think Jesus calls us to love our enemies, turn the other cheek, and so on?

2. At first glance, the teaching in this passage doesn't make much sense—but verse 31 gives us a great summary: "Do to others as you would have them do to you." What do you find difficult about this standard Jesus presents here? (Thinking honestly about this question reveals the hidden hypocrite lurking inside all of us—so take a risk and go deep.) Why is it difficult for you to love your enemies?

3. Who are your enemies and those who take advantage of you?

4. It's easy to justify our poor treatment of others. We typically begin with something like, "They deserve it!" What does verse 37 have to say about this?

5. Are you holding a grudge against someone in your life? What is that bitterness doing to you? What do you need to do to make things right?

6. In whose best interest is it to forgive: yours or the person you forgive? Explain.

7. How can understanding Jesus' life help you live up to this standard? How will you find the strength to live up to this challenge?

8. If God loves us no matter what, why should we forgive those who hurt us?

9. Reread verses 37-38. These verses demonstrate the strong connection between the quality of our earthly relationships and the quality of our relationship with God. How does this make you feel? How can this connection help you "diagnose" your spiritual life?

10. What has forgiving other people taught you about God's forgiveness toward you? Be specific in your answer.

MINISTRY: SERVING OTHERS IN LOVE

Goal: To recognize and take advantage of opportunities to serve others

Forgiveness is never easy. But forgiveness is crucial if you're going to move forward in your faith and deepen your relationship with God. If question #2 is too deep for you right now, consider taking the action at a later time. Ask the people in your group to pray for you to have both the courage and the opportunity to act.

1. Name someone you need to forgive.

2. Try this exercise: In the quiet of your own heart, say to that person, "I forgive you; you're released from responsibility for my hurt."

   Make an effort to tell that person the same thing to his or her face. If you can't do it face-to-face, writing a letter would be the next best thing.

   When you do this, it will minister to the offender. Hang on to your thoughts about this exercise and share them with a partner when you get to the surrender section of this session.

3. Why might this be an act of ministry to the offender?

4. Many men and women in prison are weighed down by the guilt of their crimes. You could have a tremendous ministry to prisoners by writing to them and sharing your own experience with forgiveness—pointing to God's extreme forgiveness and encouraging them to seek God's forgiveness as well. (If you're under 18, the law prohibits you from sending a letter on your own. Your youth leader can send a letter on behalf of the youth ministry. Adult leaders, if you're interested in doing this as a ministry project, see page 103 for more information.)

Goal: To consider how the truths from this session might be applied to your relationships with unbelievers

Read the following story and answer the questions that follow.

Tom sobbed when he heard his wife's words: "I found another man. I'm leaving you."

Through his tears he said, "I forgive you, Monica, but I don't trust you."

Monica wanted to be released without a fight. But Tom wouldn't let her go—he loved her more than that. Over many agonizing months, Monica first left the other man to repair her marriage, and then was unfaithful again.

Tom told her she had to leave the house until she was willing to work on the marriage. Again Monica decided to commit to Tom and leave the other man.

One night she told Tom she was pregnant, and it wasn't Tom's baby. It was more than Tom could bear. He struggled month after month, wondering whether he should leave his wife. He couldn't bear the thought of raising someone else's baby.

With five weeks left in the pregnancy, Tom decided to leave Monica. During a Bible study, Tom's small-group leader challenged his decision. "Tom," he said, "this baby is not some other man's. It's God's baby, and he wants you to raise it with your wife. Leave the rest to God."

Tom went home and told Monica he was committed to her and the baby. When Jacob was born, the other man came to see the child. Tom prayed to be able to love this man with Christ's love. He prayed the whole way to the hospital. When the man walked in, Tom said, "Hey, enjoy the baby. Go ahead and hold him."

The man had brought two large buddies, thinking the scene might get ugly. But it didn't. A few days later, he phoned and

asked to speak with Tom. He told Tom that never in his life had he met anyone who had handled himself in such a way. "I don't understand your Christian thing," he said, "but I am half the man you are. I want you to raise this child. You will do twice the job I could do."

A blood test later revealed that it actually wasn't the other man's baby—it was Tom and Monica's. But even if the test had turned out otherwise, Tom knew he did what Jesus would have done.

1. How does this tragic story connect with evangelism?

2. In your wildest dreams, can you imagine doing what Tom did?

3. How can forgiveness become part of your everyday life?

WORSHIP: SURRENDERING YOUR LIFE TO HONOR GOD

Goal: To focus on God's presence

1. Pair up with someone from your group and answer question # 1 in the Ministry section on page 65.

2. Together, pray about forgiveness—either in regard to a situation in which you need God's help to forgive someone or an area where you yourself need God's forgiveness.

3. End your time in prayer.

AT HOME THIS WEEK

Option 1: A Weekly Reflection

Take another self-evaluation that reflects five areas of your spiritual life (fellowship, discipleship, ministry, evangelism, and worship). See page 70.

Option 2: Daily Bible Readings

Check out the Bible reading plan on pages 122-123.

Option 3: Memory Verses

Memorize another verse from pages 127-128.

Option 4: Journaling

Choose one or more of the following options:

- Write down whatever is on your mind.
- Read your journal entry from last week and write a reflection about it.
- Respond to these questions: Why is forgiveness so difficult for me? Whom do I really need to forgive? What will forgiving this person cost me?

Option 5: Wrap It Up

Write out your answers to any questions that you didn't answer during your small group time.

LEARN A LITTLE MORE

Turn to him the other [cheek] (Luke 6:29)

Turning the other cheek hurts, but Jesus tells us we should be more concerned with doing good than with protecting ourselves or striking back. The person who turns the other cheek understands the radical standard of peace Jesus desires from his followers. This is a very mature response and requires trusting that God's way is the right way.

Remember: Jesus never tells us to turn *someone else's* cheek! We should never shut our eyes to abuse directed toward others; we must get involved and protect with an attitude of love for everyone involved.

A good measure, pressed down, shaken together and running over, will be poured into your lap (6:38)[1]

This illustration made sense to a farming society: "The image here is of a measuring container into which as much grain as possible is packed; it is then shaken to allow the grain to settle, and more is poured in till the container overflows."

FOR DEEPER STUDY ON YOUR OWN

1. What does Paul say in Romans 12:9-21 about loving our enemies? How do his views explain or expand what Jesus said?

2. Read Luke 17:3-4. What guidelines for forgiveness does Jesus offer?

3. In Ephesians 4:25-5:2, Paul discusses some related attitudes he sees as essential for a Christian community. What are those attitudes?

4. Why do you think both Jesus and Paul identified anger and forgiveness as core issues for Christians to address in their lives?

[1] Keener, C. S. & InterVarsity Press (1993). *The IVP Bible Background Commentary: New Testament* (Luke 6:38).

A WEEKLY REFLECTION

Take a minute to reflect on how well you've been doing in the following five areas of your spiritual life this week—a 10 means you did an amazing job. This reflection can serve as a spiritual gauge to help you consider some very important areas. This is for your personal evaluation and growth; it's NOT a test—no one else needs to see it.

FELLOWSHIP: CONNECTING YOUR HEART TO OTHERS

How well did I connect with other Christians?

1　2　3　4　5　6　7　8　9　10

DISCIPLESHIP: GROWING TO BE LIKE JESUS

How well did I take steps to grow spiritually and deepen my faith on my own?

1　2　3　4　5　6　7　8　9　10

MINISTRY: SERVING OTHERS IN LOVE

How well did I recognize opportunities to serve others and follow through?

1　2　3　4　5　6　7　8　9　10

EVANGELISM: SHARING YOUR STORY AND GOD'S STORY

How well did I engage in spiritual conversations with non-Christians?

1　2　3　4　5　6　7　8　9　10

WORSHIP: SURRENDERING YOUR LIFE TO HONOR GOD

How well did I focus on God's presence and honor him with my life? Was my relationship with God a primary focus?

1 2 3 4 5 6 7 8 9 10

When you finish, celebrate the areas where you feel good and consider how you can use those strengths to help others in their journey to be more like Jesus. You might also want to take time to identify some potential areas for growth.

SESSION 6

CROSS-SHAPED LOVE

 LEADERS, READ PAGE 86.

Heather wasn't really Kimmie's friend. Well, sort of...but only by association with her parents. The girls' parents were in a Bible study together, and Kimmie and Heather often attended the same functions. It's just that Heather didn't want her "real" friends to think that she associated with Kimmie, even when social situations forced it.

Heather didn't want to be connected to a girl who talked funny and walked with a limp. Kimmie was nice, but Heather didn't think she'd fit in with her friends at school. So on campus they didn't hang out, although during their parents' Bible study at Heather's house the girls would watch TV and eat the leftover desserts. Away from school, they got along fine and always had a decent time together. But at school Heather never went out of her way to greet or connect with Kimmie.

Kimmie offered Heather rides home from school, but Heather always refused because she didn't want to be seen with Kimmie. Although Heather felt guilty because she knew the way she treated Kimmie was wrong, her feelings weren't strong enough to change her actions. She knew she was being unfair and unkind, but Heather was just so embarrassed about bringing Kimmie along with her other friends. She didn't know how they would react to Kimmie; she wasn't even sure how she felt about having a "different" friend.

One night, Heather invited her school friends over to study on the same night as her parents' Bible study. When she realized Kimmie would be there too, she started to worry. But when the other girls came over and met Kimmie, they didn't think anything was weird at all. They all ate the leftover desserts and studied together—even Kimmie. No one said anything negative about Kimmie, either. It was no big deal, and Heather was relieved. As they all left to go home, Kimmie thanked Heather for introducing her to the girls and for her thoughtfulness to include her that evening.

When Heather went to bed, she couldn't believe that she had worried so much over an imaginary situation that never materialized. She felt embarrassed by her thoughtless and selfish actions and asked God to forgive her. She was sorry that she cared so much about her standing among her friends that she hadn't really accepted Kimmie apart from Bible study nights. That night, her friends taught Heather a great lesson about acceptance and about the sinfulness lurking in her own heart.

In this final session you will look at the passion Jesus has for you that resulted in his death and how much he loves you…despite your "differences."

♥ FELLOWSHIP: CONNECTING YOUR HEART TO OTHERS

Goal: To share about your life and listen attentively to others, caring about what they share

Choose one of the following options to get your group talking:

1. Based on the story that opened this chapter, are you more like Kimmie or Heather? Why?

2. Which of the previous five sessions has been the most helpful to you?

   a. Making sacrifices for others
   b. Showing up and taking action for someone in need
   c. Treating someone who's difficult to love with warmth rather than judgment
   d. Telling someone a difficult truth with a tender heart
   e. Forgiving someone who hurts you

3. Share one highlight you've experienced with this group or with this book.

DISCIPLESHIP: GROWING TO BE LIKE JESUS

Goal: To explore God's Word, gain biblical knowledge, and make personal applications

Being a Christian means many things—community, beliefs, habits—but at the center of it all stands the cross. Jesus lived a powerful life and influenced many with his teaching, miracles, and friendship. But the most powerful thing Jesus did happened on the cross. In this section, you're going to read about the death of Jesus to consider again what it means for your life.

Before you read this passage, imagine yourself at the scene of this historical event. Picture what it would have been like to be at the cross and the empty tomb.

Read Matthew 27:32-56. **(If you don't have a Bible, the passage is on pages 97-98.)**

1. Read this passage slowly—either silently or aloud—and then take a moment of silence to reflect on its meaning for your life.

2. Why do you think Jesus was criticized and ridiculed by his enemies? They got what they wanted; Jesus was sentenced to death. Why did they still have to speak against him?

3. If Jesus had come down from the cross like the religious leaders challenged (verse 42-43), do you think that would have caused them to believe in him? If Jesus was all about building faith in people, why didn't he come down off the cross?

4. Why do you think Jesus had to die on the cross? Since God is all-powerful and loving, why didn't God just forgive everyone instead of subjecting Jesus—his own son—to a horrible death?

5. According to this passage, what role did women play in Jesus' ministry?

6. Why did Jesus say that God had forsaken him (verse 46)?

7. In your own words, what is the message of the cross? Why does the cross matter for us today, more than 2,000 years later?

8. How has the cross helped you personally? Describe a recent time in your life where the power of the cross gave you real help.

MINISTRY: SERVING OTHERS IN LOVE

Goal: To recognize and take advantage of opportunities to serve others

The idea of loving others in extreme ways like Jesus did is pretty tough to understand—much less carry out—today. Knowing you probably won't die on a cross for someone else, consider a lesser act of love that might also be extreme.

1. What's the most extreme act of love you could show someone this week?

2. What keeps you from showing that type of love on a regular basis?

EVANGELISM: SHARING YOUR STORY AND GOD'S STORY

Goal: To consider how the truths from this session might be applied to your relationships with unbelievers

The cross is a key symbol for Christians, and if you're a follower of Jesus, the cross represents something foundational to your faith. You can't grow up spiritually without at some point considering the power and the meaning of the cross.

1. Read about the cross and crucifixion on page 105. After reading the horror behind death on the cross, share how you feel about crucifixion.

2. Many people wear crosses as jewelry, but not many really understand the significance behind what they're wearing. Without sounding corny, how might you casually transition your conversation about someone's jewelry to a conversation about what Jesus did on the cross?

3. This idea is a little more risky. Stage a role-play with a

few people from your group. Two of you play the role of non-Christians interested in spiritual things. The third person will explain the message of the cross. The conversation begins with one of the non-Christians asking, "So, why did Jesus die on the cross anyway?" The Christian offers answers, and the non-Christians can ask questions and challenge the answers. Everyone then debriefs about what they learned from the role-play. (Be sure you don't force group members to play roles when they don't feel comfortable. Allow people to volunteer rather than assigning roles.)

⊼ WORSHIP: SURRENDERING YOUR LIFE TO HONOR GOD

Goal: To focus on God's presence

Before you finish this session, take some time to personalize the meaning of the cross for your life.

1. Create your own acronym/acrostic using the word *cross*. There's no right or wrong way to do this. Just think about the word, its significance, and its meaning to you personally. Then either write sentences or key words or phrases that mean something to you. (See the example below.)

Christ	C
Resurrection	R
Obeyed God	O
Sacrifice	S
Sins	S

Since this is the last time your group will be together with this particular book as your guide, make sure you take some time to discuss what will happen to your group next. If you want to continue to study the incredible life and teachings of Jesus, there are a total of six books in this series.

2. Before you close with an extended time of prayer, take some time to read the key verses on pages 98-100. Use the words of the verses to help you craft your prayer… or simply read the Scriptures aloud as you pray.

AT HOME THIS WEEK

Option 1: A Weekly Reflection

Take another self-evaluation that reflects five areas of your spiritual life (fellowship, discipleship, ministry, evangelism, and worship). See page 82.

Option 2: Daily Bible Readings

Check out the Bible reading plan on pages 122-123.

Option 3: Memory Verses

Memorize another verse from pages 127-128.

Option 4: Journaling

Choose one or more of the following options:

- Write down whatever is on your mind.
- Read your journal entry from last week and write a reflection about it.
- Complete these partial statements: (1) Jesus' death on the cross means _____ (2) Jesus' death on the cross means _____ to me; (3) Jesus' death on the cross means _____ for all humanity.

Option 5: Wrap It Up

Write out your answers to any questions that you didn't answer during your small group time.

LEARN A LITTLE MORE

"You who are going to destroy the temple and build it in three days" (Matthew 27:40)

Jesus' accusers mocked him with his own words. John 2:19-21 reads, "Jesus answered them, 'Destroy this temple, and I will raise it again in three days.' The Jews replied, 'It has taken forty-six years to build this temple, and you are going to raise it in three days?' But the temple he had spoken of was his body."

...sixth hour until the ninth hour... (27:45)
This means from noon until 3 p.m.

Elijah (27:47)
Elijah was a great prophet and hero from the Old Testament. The Bible says he never died because he was taken directly to heaven (See 1 Kings 17-19,21 and 2 Kings 1-2). Many people believed he would return when the Messiah came.

Curtain of the Temple (27:50)
"The innermost screen...was used to divide the innermost sacred space from the outer sanctum (Exodus 35:12; 39:34; Numbers 3:31; 4:5). This screen, supported by four pillars, thus shielded the ark [of the covenant] from the view of priests ministering to the items in the outer sanctum."[1] (Exodus 40:3, 21)

Centurion (27:54)
A centurion commanded 100 soldiers in a Roman legion (a legion contained 3,000 soldiers). "The ordinary duties of the centurion were to drill his men, inspect their arms, food and clothing, and to command them in the camp and in the field."[2] Sometimes centurions were given special duties that separated them from their legions.

My God, my God, why have you forsaken me? (27:46)
Jesus was quoting Psalm 22:1. In this Psalm, David vividly describes his feelings of separation from God in the midst of trouble at the hands of his enemies. This psalm also contains the prophecy concerning the soldiers who took Jesus' garments (verse 18).

In this moment, Jesus bore the sins of the world and experienced the full punishment of sin: separation from God

---

[1] Freedman, D. N. (1996, c1992). *The Anchor Bible Dictionary*. New York: Doubleday.
[2] from the *International Standard Bible Encyclopedia*.

(see 2 Corinthians 5:21). God the Father momentarily left his Son because of the sin he bore. It was agonizing for Jesus to be separated from his Father—in all eternity he had never experienced this.

In this Scripture we come face to face with one of the mysteries of Jesus. He was fully God, fully united with God—yet for this moment he was separated from God. We call this a mystery because we cannot adequately explain or understand it. (How could God be separated from himself?)

There is a practical side in understanding why Jesus quoted Psalm 22. First of all, we shouldn't be afraid to express ourselves when we feel separated from God. This isn't necessarily an indication of spiritual immaturity, and it definitely doesn't throw your salvation into question. Doubts, fears, and feelings of loneliness are all wrapped up in what it means to be human. The Bible affirms this: David, one of the greatest kings of Israel, faced these same feelings. It's helpful to be acquainted with the Psalms, for they contain many instances of real emotion that often express our feelings better than we can on our own!

FOR DEEPER STUDY ON YOUR OWN

1. Compare Psalm 22 to Jesus' experience on the cross. Which verses reflect what Jesus may have been thinking and feeling?

2. Read Romans 3:21-31. Why does Jesus' death "justify" us—that is, make God declare us "not guilty" for our sins?

3. Read Philippians 2:1-13. How did Paul think the cross should affect the way we live day to day?

4. What parallels do you see between Isaiah's prophecy

of the suffering servant (Isaiah 52:13-53:12) and what actually happened to Jesus?

5. For Old Testament background on the idea of sacrifice for payment of sin, see Leviticus 16. What was the point of blood sacrifice?

A WEEKLY REFLECTION

Take a minute to reflect on how well you've been doing in the following five areas of your spiritual life this week—a 10 means you did an amazing job. This reflection can serve as a spiritual gauge to help you consider some very important areas. This is for your personal evaluation and growth; it's NOT a test—no one else needs to see it.

FELLOWSHIP: CONNECTING YOUR HEART TO OTHERS'
How well did I connect with other Christians?

1   2   3   4   5   6   7   8   9   10

DISCIPLESHIP: GROWING TO BE LIKE JESUS
How well did I take steps to grow spiritually and deepen my faith on my own?

1   2   3   4   5   6   7   8   9   10

MINISTRY: SERVING OTHERS IN LOVE
How well did I recognize opportunities to serve others and follow through?

1   2   3   4   5   6   7   8   9   10

EVANGELISM: SHARING YOUR STORY AND GOD'S STORY

How well did I engage in spiritual conversations with non-Christians?

1   2   3   4   5   6   7   8   9   10

WORSHIP: SURRENDERING YOUR LIFE TO HONOR GOD

How well did I focus on God's presence and honor him with my life? Was my relationship with God a primary focus?

1   2   3   4   5   6   7   8   9   10

When you finish, celebrate the areas where you feel good and consider how you can use those strengths to help others in their journey to be more like Jesus. You might also want to take time to identify some potential areas for growth.

APPENDICES

Small Group Leader Checklist — 86

For Small Group Leaders: How to Best Use This Material — 87

Scripture Passages — 91

I Just Want to Encourage You! — 101

About Prison Fellowship: An Option for Session 5 — 103

What Was Crucifixion? — 105

Who Is Jesus? — 106

A Summary of the Life of Jesus — 108

Small Group Roster — 110

How to Keep Your Group from Becoming a Clique — 111

Spiritual Health Assessment — 113

Daily Bible Readings — 122

How to Study the Bible On Your Own — 124

Memory Verses — 127

Journaling: Snapshots of Your Heart — 129

Journal Pages — 132

Praying in Your Small Group — 138

Prayer Request Guidelines — 140

Prayer Options — 142

Prayer Request Log — 144

EXPERIENCING CHRIST TOGETHER for a Year — 150

About the Authors — 152

SMALL GROUP LEADER CHECKLIST

- Read through "For Small Group Leaders: How to Best Use this Material" (see pages 87-90). This is very important—familiarizing yourself with it will help you understand content and how to best manage your time.

- Read through all the questions in the session that you'll be leading. The questions are a guide for you to help students grow spiritually. Think through which questions are best for your group. Remember, no curriculum author knows your students better than you do! Just a small amount of preparation on your part will help you manage the time you'll have with your group. Based on the amount of time you'll have in your small group, circle the questions you will discuss as a group. Decide what (if anything) you will assign at the end of the session (things like homework, snacks, group project, and so on).

- Remember that the questions in this book don't always have obvious, neat, tidy answers. Some are purposely written to cause good discussion without a specific "right" answer. Often questions (and answers) will lead to more questions.

- Make sure you have enough books for your students and a few extra in case your students invite friends. (Note: It's vital for your group to decide during the first session whether you can invite friends to join your group. If not, encourage your group to think of friends they can invite if you go through the next EXPERIENCING CHRIST TOGETHER book in this series.)

- Read the material included in this appendix. It's filled with information that will benefit your group and your student ministry. This appendix alone is a great reference for students—familiarize yourself with the tools here so you can offer them to students.

- Submit your leadership and your group to God. Ask God to provide you with insight into how to lead your group, patience to do so, and courage to speak truth in love when needed.

FOR SMALL GROUP LEADERS: HOW TO BEST USE THIS MATERIAL

This book was written more as a guidebook than a workbook. In most workbooks, you're supposed to answer every question and fill in all the blanks. In this book, there are lots of questions and plenty of blank space. Explain to your students that this isn't a school workbook—they're not graded on how much they've written.

The number-one rule for this curriculum is that there are no rules apart from the ones you decide to use. Every small group is unique and will figure out its own style and system. (The exception is when the lead youth worker establishes a guideline for all the groups to follow. In that case, respect your leader's guidelines.)

If you need a guide to get you started until you navigate your own way, here's a way to adapt the material for a 60-minute session.

Introduction (4 minutes)

Begin each session with one student reading the Small Group Covenant (see page 18). This becomes a constant reminder of why you'll be doing what you're doing. Then have another student read the opening paragraphs of the session you'll be discussing. Allow different students to take turns reading these two opening pieces.

Connecting (10 minutes)

This section can take 45 minutes if you're not careful! You'll need to stay on task to keep this segment short—consider giving students a specific amount of time and holding them to it. It's always better to leave students wanting more time for discussion than to leave them bored.

Growing (25 minutes)

Read God's Word and work through the questions you think will be best for your group. This section definitely has more questions than you're able to discuss in the allotted time. Before the small group begins, take some time to read through the questions and choose the best ones for your group. You may also want to add questions of your own. If someone forgets a Bible, we've provided the Scripture passages for each session in the appendix.

The questions in this book don't always have obvious, neat, tidy answers. Some are purposely written to cause good discussion without a specific "right" answer. Often questions (and answers) will lead to more questions.

If your small group is biblically mature, this section won't be too difficult. However, if your group struggles with these questions, make sure you sift through them and focus on the few questions that will help drive the message home. Also, you might want to encourage your group to answer the remaining questions on their own.

Serving and Sharing (10 minutes)

If you're pressed for time, you may choose to skip one of these two sections. If you do need to skip one due to time constraints, group members can finish the section on their own during the week. Don't feel guilty about passing over a section. **One of the strengths of this material is the built-in, intentional repetition in every session. You will have other opportunities to discuss that biblical purpose.** (Again, that's the main reason for spending a few minutes before your group meets to read through all the questions and pick the best ones for your group.)

Surrendering (10 minutes)

We always want to end the lesson with a focus on God and a specific time of prayer. You'll have several options, but feel free to default to your group's comfort level.

Closing Challenge (1 minute)

Encourage students to pick one option each from the "At Home This Week" section to complete on their own. The more students initiate and develop the habit of spending time with God, the healthier their spiritual journeys will be. We've found that students have plenty of unanswered questions that they will consider on their own time. **Keep in mind that the main goal of this book is building spiritual growth in community—not to get your students to answer every question correctly.** Remember that this is your small group, your time, and the questions will always be there. Use them, ignore them, or assign them for personal study during the week—but don't feel pressure to follow this curriculum exactly or "grade" your group's biblical knowledge.

Finally, remember that questions are a great way to get students connected to one another and God's Word. You don't have to have all the answers.

Suggestions for Existing Small Groups

If your small group has been meeting for a while and you've already established comfortable relationships, you can jump right into the material. But make sure you take the following actions, even if you're a well-established group:

- Read through the "Small Group Covenant" on page 18 and make additions or adjustments as necessary.

- Read the "Prayer Request Guidelines" together (page 140). You can maximize the group's time by following them.

- Before each meeting, consider whether you'll assign material to be completed (or at least thought through) before your next meeting.

- Familiarize yourself with all the "At Home This Week" options at the end of each session. They are explained in detail near the end of Session 1 (page 26), and then briefly summarized at the end of the other five sessions.

Although handling business like this can seem cumbersome or unnecessary to an existing group, these foundational steps can save you from headaches later on because you took the time to create an environment conducive to establishing deep relationships.

Suggestions for New Small Groups

If your group is meeting together for the first time, jumping right into the first session may not be your best option. You may want to meet as a group before you begin going through the book so you can get to know each other better. To prepare for the first gathering, read and follow the "Suggestions for Existing Groups" mentioned previously.

Spend some time getting to know each other with icebreaker questions. Several are listed here. Pick one or two that will work best for your group or use your own. The goal is to break ground so you can plant the seeds of healthy relationships.

1. What's your name, school, grade, and favorite class in school? (Picking your least favorite class is too easy.)

2. Tell the group a brief (basic) history of your family. What's your family life like? How many brothers and sisters do you have? Which family members are you closest to?

3. What's one thing about yourself that you really like?

4. Everyone has little personality quirks—traits that make each one of us unique. What are yours?

5. Why did you choose to be a part of this small group?

6. What do you hope to get out of this small group? How do you expect it to help you?

7. What do you think it will take to make our small group work well?

Need some teaching help?

Companion DVDs are available for each EXPERIENCING CHRIST TOGETHER book. These DVDs contain teaching segments you can use to supplement each session. Play them before your discussion begins or just prior to the "Discipleship" section in each session. The DVDs aren't required, but they are a great complement and supplement to the small group material. These are available from www.youthspecialties.com.

SCRIPTURE PASSAGES

Session 1

John 15:9-17

[9]As the Father has loved me, so have I loved you. Now remain in my love. [10]If you obey my commands, you will remain in my love, just as I have obeyed my Father's commands and remain in his love. [11]I have told you this so that my joy may be in you and that your joy may be complete. [12]My command is this: Love each other as I have loved you. [13]Greater love has no one than this, that he lay down his life for his friends. [14]You are my friends if you do what I command. [15]I no longer call you servants, because a servant does not know his master's business. Instead, I have called you friends, for everything that I learned from my Father I have made known to you. [16]You did not choose me, but I chose you and appointed you to go and bear fruit—fruit that will last. Then the Father will give you whatever you ask in my name. [17]This is my command: Love each other."

Psalm 139

[1]O Lord, you have searched me
   and you know me.
[2]You know when I sit and when I rise;
   you perceive my thoughts from afar.
[3]You discern my going out and my lying down;
   you are familiar with all my ways.
[4]Before a word is on my tongue
   you know it completely, O Lord.

[5]You hem me in—behind and before;
   you have laid your hand upon me.
[6]Such knowledge is too wonderful for me,
   too lofty for me to attain.

[7]Where can I go from your Spirit?
   Where can I flee from your presence?
[8]If I go up to the heavens, you are there;
   if I make my bed in the depths, you are there.
[9]If I rise on the wings of the dawn,
   if I settle on the far side of the sea,

¹⁰even there your hand will guide me,
  your right hand will hold me fast.

¹¹If I say, "Surely the darkness will hide me
  and the light become night around me,"
¹²even the darkness will not be dark to you;
  the night will shine like the day,
  for darkness is as light to you.

¹³For you created my inmost being;
  you knit me together in my mother's womb.
¹⁴I praise you because I am fearfully and wonderfully made;
  your works are wonderful,
  I know that full well.
¹⁵My frame was not hidden from you
  when I was made in the secret place.
When I was woven together in the depths of the earth,
¹⁶your eyes saw my unformed body.
All the days ordained for me
  were written in your book
  before one of them came to be.

¹⁷How precious to me are your thoughts, O God!
  How vast is the sum of them!
¹⁸Were I to count them,
  they would outnumber the grains of sand.
When I awake,
  I am still with you.

¹⁹If only you would slay the wicked, O God!
  Away from me, you bloodthirsty men!
²⁰They speak of you with evil intent;
  your adversaries misuse your name.
²¹Do I not hate those who hate you, O Lord,
  and abhor those who rise up against you?
²²I have nothing but hatred for them;
  I count them my enemies.

²³Search me, O God, and know my heart;
  test me and know my anxious thoughts.
²⁴See if there is any offensive way in me,
  and lead me in the way everlasting.

Session 2

John 11:1-44

¹Now a man named Lazarus was sick. He was from Bethany, the village of Mary and her sister Martha. ²This Mary, whose brother Lazarus now lay sick, was the same one who poured perfume on the Lord and wiped his feet with her hair. ³So the sisters sent word to Jesus, "Lord, the one you love is sick."

⁴When he heard this, Jesus said, "This sickness will not end in death. No, it is for God's glory so that God's Son may be glorified through it." ⁵Jesus loved Martha and her sister and Lazarus. ⁶Yet when he heard that Lazarus was sick, he stayed where he was two more days.

⁷Then he said to his disciples, "Let us go back to Judea."

⁸"But Rabbi," they said, "a short while ago the Jews tried to stone you, and yet you are going back there?"

⁹Jesus answered, "Are there not twelve hours of daylight? A man who walks by day will not stumble, for he sees by this world's light. ¹⁰It is when he walks by night that he stumbles, for he has no light."

¹¹After he had said this, he went on to tell them, "Our friend Lazarus has fallen asleep; but I am going there to wake him up."

¹²His disciples replied, "Lord, if he sleeps, he will get better." ¹³Jesus had been speaking of his death, but his disciples thought he meant natural sleep.

¹⁴So then he told them plainly, "Lazarus is dead, ¹⁵and for your sake I am glad I was not there, so that you may believe. But let us go to him."

¹⁶Then Thomas (called Didymus) said to the rest of the disciples, "Let us also go, that we may die with him."

¹⁷On his arrival, Jesus found that Lazarus had already been in the tomb for four days. ¹⁸Bethany was less than two miles from Jerusalem, ¹⁹and many Jews had come to Martha and Mary to comfort them in the loss of their brother. ²⁰When Martha heard that Jesus was coming, she went out to meet him, but Mary stayed at home.

²¹"Lord," Martha said to Jesus, "if you had been here, my brother would not have died. ²²But I know that even now God will give you whatever you ask."

²³Jesus said to her, "Your brother will rise again."

²⁴Martha answered, "I know he will rise again in the resurrection at the last day."

²⁵Jesus said to her, "I am the resurrection and the life. He who believes in me will live, even though he dies; ²⁶and whoever lives and believes in me will never die. Do you believe this?"

²⁷"Yes, Lord," she told him, "I believe that you are the Christ, the Son of God, who was to come into the world."

²⁸And after she had said this, she went back and called her sister Mary aside. "The Teacher is here," she said, "and is asking for you." ²⁹When Mary heard this, she got up quickly and went to him. ³⁰Now Jesus had not yet entered the village, but was still at the place where Martha had met him. ³¹When the Jews who had been with Mary in the house, comforting her, noticed how quickly she got up and went out, they followed her, supposing she was going to the tomb to mourn there.

³²When Mary reached the place where Jesus was and saw him, she fell at his feet and said, "Lord, if you had been here, my brother would not have died."

³³When Jesus saw her weeping, and the Jews who had come along with her also weeping, he was deeply moved in spirit and troubled. ³⁴"Where have you laid him?" he asked.

"Come and see, Lord," they replied.

³⁵Jesus wept.

³⁶Then the Jews said, "See how he loved him!"

³⁷But some of them said, "Could not he who opened the eyes of the blind man have kept this man from dying?"

³⁸Jesus, once more deeply moved, came to the tomb. It was a cave with a stone laid across the entrance. ³⁹"Take away the stone," he said.

"But, Lord," said Martha, the sister of the dead man, "by this time there is a bad odor, for he has been there four days."

⁴⁰Then Jesus said, "Did I not tell you that if you believed, you would see the glory of God?"

⁴¹So they took away the stone. Then Jesus looked up and said, "Father, I thank you that you have heard me. ⁴²I knew that you always hear me, but

I said this for the benefit of the people standing here, that they may believe that you sent me."

[43]When he had said this, Jesus called in a loud voice, "Lazarus, come out!" [44]The dead man came out, his hands and feet wrapped with strips of linen, and a cloth around his face.

Jesus said to them, "Take off the grave clothes and let him go."

Session 3

John 8:1-11

[1]But Jesus went to the Mount of Olives. [2]At dawn he appeared again in the temple courts, where all the people gathered around him, and he sat down to teach them. [3]The teachers of the law and the Pharisees brought in a woman caught in adultery. They made her stand before the group [4]and said to Jesus, "Teacher, this woman was caught in the act of adultery. [5]In the Law Moses commanded us to stone such women. Now what do you say?" [6]They were using this question as a trap, in order to have a basis for accusing him.

But Jesus bent down and started to write on the ground with his finger. [7]When they kept on questioning him, he straightened up and said to them, "If any one of you is without sin, let him be the first to throw a stone at her." [8]Again he stooped down and wrote on the ground.

[9]At this, those who heard began to go away one at a time, the older ones first, until only Jesus was left, with the woman still standing there. [10]Jesus straightened up and asked her, "Woman, where are they? Has no one condemned you?"

[11]"No one, sir," she said.

"Then neither do I condemn you," Jesus declared. "Go now and leave your life of sin."

Session 4

Matthew 16:13-28

[13]When Jesus came to the region of Caesarea Philippi, he asked his disciples, "Who do people say the Son of Man is?"

¹⁴They replied, "Some say John the Baptist; others say Elijah; and still others, Jeremiah or one of the prophets."

¹⁵"But what about you?" he asked. "Who do you say I am?"

¹⁶Simon Peter answered, "You are the Christ, the Son of the living God."

¹⁷Jesus replied, "Blessed are you, Simon son of Jonah, for this was not revealed to you by man, but by my Father in heaven. ¹⁸And I tell you that you are Peter, and on this rock I will build my church, and the gates of Hades will not overcome it. ¹⁹I will give you the keys of the kingdom of heaven; whatever you bind on earth will be bound in heaven, and whatever you loose on earth will be loosed in heaven." ²⁰Then he warned his disciples not to tell anyone that he was the Christ.

²¹From that time on Jesus began to explain to his disciples that he must go to Jerusalem and suffer many things at the hands of the elders, chief priests and teachers of the law, and that he must be killed and on the third day be raised to life.

²²Peter took him aside and began to rebuke him. "Never, Lord!" he said. "This shall never happen to you!"

²³Jesus turned and said to Peter, "Get behind me, Satan! You are a stumbling block to me; you do not have in mind the things of God, but the things of men."

²⁴Then Jesus said to his disciples, "If anyone would come after me, he must deny himself and take up his cross and follow me. ²⁵For whoever wants to save his life will lose it, but whoever loses his life for me will find it. ²⁶What good will it be for a man if he gains the whole world, yet forfeits his soul? Or what can a man give in exchange for his soul? ²⁷For the Son of Man is going to come in his Father's glory with his angels, and then he will reward each person according to what he has done. ²⁸I tell you the truth, some who are standing here will not taste death before they see the Son of Man coming in his kingdom."

Session 5

Luke 6:27-38

²⁷"But I tell you who hear me: Love your enemies, do good to those who hate you, ²⁸bless those who curse you, pray for those who mistreat you. ²⁹If

someone strikes you on one cheek, turn to him the other also. If some-one takes your cloak, do not stop him from taking your tunic. [30]Give to everyone who asks you, and if anyone takes what belongs to you, do not demand it back. [31]Do to others as you would have them do to you.

[32]"If you love those who love you, what credit is that to you? Even 'sinners' love those who love them. [33]And if you do good to those who are good to you, what credit is that to you? Even 'sinners' do that. [34]And if you lend to those from whom you expect repayment, what credit is that to you? Even 'sinners' lend to 'sinners,' expecting to be repaid in full. [35]But love your enemies, do good to them, and lend to them without expecting to get anything back. Then your reward will be great, and you will be sons of the Most High, because he is kind to the ungrateful and wicked. [36]Be merciful, just as your Father is merciful.

[37]"Do not judge, and you will not be judged. Do not condemn, and you will not be condemned. Forgive, and you will be forgiven. [38]Give, and it will be given to you. A good measure, pressed down, shaken to-gether and running over, will be poured into your lap. For with the mea-sure you use, it will be measured to you."

Session 6

Matthew 27:32-56

[32]As they were going out, they met a man from Cyrene, named Simon, and they forced him to carry the cross. [33]They came to a place called Golgotha (which means The Place of the Skull). [34]There they offered Jesus wine to drink, mixed with gall; but after tasting it, he refused to drink it. [35]When they had crucified him, they divided up his clothes by casting lots. [36]And sitting down, they kept watch over him there. [37]Above his head they placed the written charge against him: this is Jesus, the king of the Jews. [38]Two robbers were crucified with him, one on his right and one on his left. [39]Those who passed by hurled insults at him, shaking their heads [40]and saying, "You who are going to destroy the temple and build it in three days, save yourself! Come down from the cross, if you are the Son of God!"

[41]In the same way the chief priests, the teachers of the law and the elders mocked him. [42]"He saved others," they said, "but he can't save himself! He's the King of Israel! Let him come down now from the cross, and we will believe in him. [43]He trusts in God. Let God rescue him now

How do we hurt God?

if he wants him, for he said, 'I am the Son of God.'" ⁴⁴In the same way the robbers who were crucified with him also heaped insults on him.

⁴⁵From the sixth hour until the ninth hour darkness came over all the land. ⁴⁶About the ninth hour Jesus cried out in a loud voice, "Eloi, Eloi, lama sabachthani?"—which means, "My God, my God, why have you forsaken me?"

⁴⁷When some of those standing there heard this, they said, "He's calling Elijah."

⁴⁸Immediately one of them ran and got a sponge. He filled it with wine vinegar, put it on a stick, and offered it to Jesus to drink. ⁴⁹The rest said, "Now leave him alone. Let's see if Elijah comes to save him."

⁵⁰And when Jesus had cried out again in a loud voice, he gave up his spirit.

⁵¹At that moment the curtain of the temple was torn in two from top to bottom. The earth shook and the rocks split. ⁵²The tombs broke open and the bodies of many holy people who had died were raised to life. ⁵³They came out of the tombs, and after Jesus' resurrection they went into the holy city and appeared to many people.

⁵⁴When the centurion and those with him who were guarding Jesus saw the earthquake and all that had happened, they were terrified, and exclaimed, "Surely he was the Son of God!"

⁵⁵Many women were there, watching from a distance. They had followed Jesus from Galilee to care for his needs. ⁵⁶Among them were Mary Magdalene, Mary the mother of James and Joses, and the mother of Zebedee's sons.

(Key verses for Worship, question #2)

1 Corinthians 1:18

For the message of the cross is foolishness to those who are perishing, but to us who are being saved it is the power of God

Galatians 6:12-14

¹²Those who want to make a good impression outwardly are trying to compel you to be circumcised. The only reason they do this is to avoid being

persecuted for the cross of Christ. [13]Not even those who are circumcised obey the law, yet they want you to be circumcised that they may boast about your flesh. [14]May I never boast except in the cross of our Lord Jesus Christ, through which the world has been crucified to me, and I to the world.

Ephesians 2:14-18

[14]For he himself is our peace, who has made the two one and has destroyed the barrier, the dividing wall of hostility, [15]by abolishing in his flesh the law with its commandments and regulations. His purpose was to create in himself one new man out of the two, thus making peace, [16]and in this one body to reconcile both of them to God through the cross, by which he put to death their hostility. [17]He came and preached peace to you who were far away and peace to those who were near. [18]For through him we both have access to the Father by one Spirit.

Philippians 2:8

And being found in appearance as a man, he humbled himself and became obedient to death—even death on a cross!

Philippians 3:18

For, as I have often told you before and now say again even with tears, many live as enemies of the cross of Christ.

Colossians 1:19-22

[19]For God was pleased to have all his fullness dwell in him, [20]and through him to reconcile to himself all things, whether things on earth or things in heaven, by making peace through his blood, shed on the cross. [21]Once you were alienated from God and were enemies in your minds because of your evil behavior. [22]But now he has reconciled you by Christ's physical body through death to present you holy in his sight, without blemish and free from accusation...

Colossians 2:13-15

[13]When you were dead in your sins and in the uncircumcision of your sinful nature, God made you alive with Christ. He forgave us all our sins, [14]having canceled the written code, with its regulations, that was against us and that stood opposed to us; he took it away, nailing it to the cross. [15]And having disarmed the powers and authorities, he made a public spectacle of them, triumphing over them by the cross.

Hebrews 12:2-3

²Let us fix our eyes on Jesus, the author and perfecter of our faith, who for the joy set before him endured the cross, scorning its shame, and sat down at the right hand of the throne of God. ³Consider him who endured such opposition from sinful men, so that you will not grow weary and lose heart.

I JUST WANT TO ENCOURAGE YOU!

ABOUT PRISON FELLOWSHIP

AN OPTION FOR SESSION 5

Prison Fellowship (an organization started by Chuck Colson) partners with local churches across the country to minister to people whom society often scorns and neglects: prisoners, ex-prisoners, and their families. God, unlike the world, has always chosen to identify closest with those who are isolated and broken.

> *For I was hungry and you gave me something to eat, I was thirsty and you gave me something to drink, I was a stranger and you invited me in, I needed clothes and you clothed me, I was sick and you looked after me, I was in prison, and you came to visit me...I tell you the truth, whatever you did for one of the least of these brothers of mine, you did for me. (Matthew 25:35-36, 40)*

Prison Fellowship reaches out to prisoners...as an act of service to Jesus Christ and as a contribution to restoring peace to our cities and communities endangered by crime. The best way to transform our communities is to transform the people within those communities—and truly restorative change comes only through a relationship with Jesus Christ.

Prison Fellowship asks and encourages you to make a difference in one of these prisoners' lives by becoming a Pen Pal. You can fill out an online application today. You can also request an application by writing to The Pen Pal Program, P.O. Box 2205, Ashburn, VA 20146-2205 or by calling toll-free 877-478-0100, ext. 8617.

As a Pen Pal, you can bring hope, compassion, and the gospel into a lonely environment. Prisoners are often isolated from family and friends. Often their relationship with a Christian pen pal is their only connection with the outside world. Imagine the witness to a prisoner when the only person who will write and be a friend is a Christian. Pen pals have the opportunity to engage in prison ministry without ever actually entering a prison.

> *I am writing in hopes that you may be able to help me find someone to write to, and who does not mind writing to a struggling prisoner in Texas. I am a Christian who was led here by being blind, but have since found the light. Although it is a struggle to walk with the Lord in a place where those around you would rather spit in your eye than offer a smile, I wish to find strength in correspondence and friendship. Please let me know if you can help me here. The loneliness, well...words cannot express.*

—Lonnie C., Prisoner Applying for a Pen Pal

In corresponding with inmates, I've found fulfillment and joy. They're overjoyed to receive my letters. I keep every letter they write. Many testify to what Christ has already done for them. All they have going for them is Jesus and Christians who share his love with them. They need God's love flowing through us! The Pen Pal Program gives flexibility, and regardless of schedule changes, I can always make time to write. Christian prisoners even encourage me in my faith. I value their Christian friendship and look forward to getting mail, knowing that I'll hear back from lonely, grateful inmates. In my prayers for them and my letters pointing them to my love, Christ's love, and his cross, I'm certain I'm sowing seeds. I am laying treasures in heaven for myself and changing the world for a few needy prisoners. You can too!

—Lisa D., Pen Pal Volunteer

The Prison Fellowship Web site is *www.pfm.org*

WHAT WAS CRUCIFIXION?

"Crucifixion was one of the most cruel and barbarous forms of death known to man...So dreaded was it that even in the pre-Christian era, the cares and troubles of life were often compared to a cross. The agony of the crucified victim was brought about by (1) the painful but nonfatal character of the wounds inflicted, (2) the abnormal position of the body, the slightest movement causing additional torture, and (3) the traumatic fever induced by hanging for such a long period of time...When a person is suspended by his two hands, the blood sinks rapidly into the lower extremities of the body. Within six to twelve minutes the blood pressure has dropped to half while the rate of the pulse has doubled. The heart is deprived of blood, and fainting follows. Death during crucifixion is due to heart failure. Victims of crucifixion did not generally succumb for two or three days. Death was hastened by the 'crucifragium' or the breaking of the legs. 'But when they came to Jesus and found that he was already dead, they did not break his legs' (John 19:33)." [1]

[1] "Cross," *New International Bible Dictionary,* in The Zondervan Bible Study Library CD-ROM, version 5.0 (Grand Rapids, Mich.: Zondervan, 2003).

WHO IS JESUS?

Jesus is God

The high priest said to him, "I charge you under oath by the living God: Tell us if you are the Christ, the Son of God." "Yes, it is as you say," Jesus replied. (Matthew 26:63-64)

Jesus became a person

The Word [Jesus] became flesh and made his dwelling among us. (John 1:14)

Jesus taught with authority

They were amazed at his teaching, for he taught as one who had real authority—quite unlike the teachers of religious law. (Mark 1:22)

Jesus healed the sick

Jesus went throughout Galilee, teaching in their synagogues, preaching the good news of the kingdom, and healing every disease and sickness among the people. (Matthew 4:23)

Jesus befriended outcasts

That night Matthew invited Jesus and his disciples to be his dinner guests, along with his fellow tax collectors and many other notorious sinners. The Pharisees were indignant. "Why does your teacher eat with such scum?" they asked his disciples. (Matthew 9:10-11)

Jesus got angry with religious oppressors

How terrible it will be for you teachers of religious law and you Pharisees. Hypocrites! You are like whitewashed tombs—beautiful on the outside but filled on the inside with dead people's bones and all sorts of impurity. (Matthew 23:27)

Jesus was persecuted

The chief priests and the whole Sanhedrin were looking for false evidence against Jesus so that they could put him to death. But they did not find any, though many false witnesses came forward. Finally two came forward and declared, "This fellow said, 'I am able to destroy the temple of God and rebuild it in three days.'" (Matthew 26:59-61)

Jesus was tempted in every way

… for he [Jesus] faced all of the same temptations we do… (Hebrews 4:15)

Jesus never sinned

… he [Jesus] did not sin. (Hebrews 4:15)

But you know that he [Jesus] appeared so that he might take away our sins. And in him is no sin. (1 John 3:5)

Jesus died, rose from the dead, and continues to live to this day

But Christ has indeed been raised from the dead… (1 Corinthians 15:20)

Jesus made it possible to have a relationship with God

For God so loved the world that he gave his one and only Son, that whoever believes in him shall not perish but have eternal life. For God did not send his Son into the world to condemn the world, but to save the world through him. (John 3:16-17)

Jesus can sympathize with our struggles

This High Priest of ours understands our weaknesses… (Hebrews 4:15)

Jesus loves us

May you experience the love of Christ, though it is so great you will never fully understand it. (Ephesians 3:19)

Sound good? Looking for more?

Getting to know Jesus is the best thing you can do with your life. He WON'T let you down. He knows everything about you and LOVES you more than you can imagine!

A SUMMARY OF THE LIFE OF JESUS

The Incarnation

Fully divine and fully human, God sent his son, Jesus, to the earth to bring salvation into the world for everyone who believes. *Read John 1:4.*

John the Baptist

A relative to Jesus, John was sent "to make ready a people prepared for the Lord." He called Israel to repentance and baptized people in the Jordan River. *Read Luke 3:3.*

The baptism and temptation of Jesus

After John baptized him, Jesus went into the desert for 40 days in preparation for his ministry. He faced Satan and resisted the temptation he offered by quoting Scripture. *Read Matthew 4:4.*

Jesus begins his ministry

The world's most influential person taught with authority, healed with compassion, and inspired with miracles. *Read Luke 4:15.*

Jesus' model of discipleship

Jesus called everyone to follow him—without reservation—and to love God and others. *Read Luke 9:23, 57-62.*

The opposition

The religious "upper class" opposed Jesus, seeking to discredit him in the eyes of the people. Jesus criticized their hypocrisy and love of recognition. *Read Matthew 23:25.*

The great "I Am"

Jesus claimed to be the bread of life; the light of the world; the good shepherd; and the way, the truth, and the life. Each of these titles reveals essential truth about who he is. *Read John 14:6.*

The great physician

His words brought conviction and comfort; his actions shouted to the world his true nature. Healing the sick, Jesus demonstrated his power and authority by helping people where they needed it most so they might accept the truth. *Read Matthew 14:14.*

The great forgiver

Humanity's deepest need is forgiveness and freedom from the guilt of the past—which separates us from God. Only God has the power to forgive, and Jesus further demonstrated his divinity by forgiving the guilty. *Read Matthew 9:6.*

The disciples

Jesus chose 12 ordinary men to change the world. They weren't rich, powerful, or influential. They had shady pasts, often made huge mistakes, and were filled with doubts. In spite of these things, Jesus used them to build his church. *Read Mark 3:14.*

The final night

On the night before his death, Jesus spent the time preparing his disciples, and he spent time alone. Obedient to the Father, Jesus was committed to go to the cross to pay the penalty for our sins. *Read Mark 14:32 ff.*

The Crucifixion

Jesus died a real death on the cross for the sins of the world. His ultimate sacrifice is something all believers should remember often. *Read John 19:30.*

The Resurrection

After dying on the cross, Jesus was raised from the dead by God's power. This miracle has never been disproved and validates everything Jesus taught. *Read 1 Corinthians 15:55.*

Want a more detailed chronology of Jesus' life and ministry on earth? Check out these two Web sites:

http://www.bookofjesus.com/bojchron.htm

http://mb-soft.com/believe/txh/gospgosp.htm

SMALL GROUP ROSTER

NAME	E-MAIL	PHONE	ADDRESS / CITY / ZIP CODE	SCHOOL/GRADE

HOW TO KEEP YOUR GROUP FROM BECOMING A CLIQUE

We all want to belong—God created us to be connected in community with one another. But the same drive that creates healthy community can also create negative community, often called a clique. A clique isn't just a group of friends—it's a group of friends uninterested in anyone outside their group. Cliques result in pain for those who are excluded.

If you read the second paragraph of the introduction (page 7), you see the words *spiritual community* used to describe your small group. If your small group becomes a clique, it's an unspiritual community. You have a clique when the biblical purpose of fellowship turns inward. That's ugly. It's the opposite of what God intended the body of Christ to be. Here's why:

- Cliques make your youth ministry look bad.

- Cliques make your small group appear immature.

- Cliques hurt the feelings of excluded people.

- Cliques contradict the value God places on each person.

- Few things are as unappealing as a youth ministry filled with cliques.

Many leaders avoid using their small groups as a way toward spiritual growth because they fear their groups will become cliques. But when they're healthy, small groups can improve your youth ministry's well-being, friendliness, and depth. The apostle Paul reminds us, "Be wise in the way you act toward outsiders; make the most of every opportunity" (Colossians 4:5).

Here are some ideas for being wise and preventing your small group from turning into a clique:

Be Aware

Learn to recognize when outsiders are uncomfortable with your group. It's easy to forget when you're an insider how bad it feels to be an outsider.

Reach Out

Once you're aware of someone feeling left out, make efforts to be friendly. Smile, shake hands, say hello, ask him or her to sit with you or your group, and ask simple yet personal questions. An outsider may come across as defensive, so be as accepting as possible.

Launch New Small Groups

Any small group with the attitude of "us four and no more" has become a clique. A time will come when your small group should launch into multiple small groups if it gets too big—because the bigger a small group gets, the less healthy it becomes. If your small group understands this, you can foster a culture of growth and fellowship.

For Students Only

Small group members expect adult leaders to confront them for acting like a clique. But instead of waiting for an adult to make the move, shock everyone by stepping up and challenging what you know is destructive. Take a risk. Be a spokesperson for your youth ministry and your student peers by leading the way. Be part of a small group that isn't cliquey and don't be afraid to challenge those who are.

SPIRITUAL HEALTH ASSESSMENT

Evaluating your spiritual journey is important—that's why we've encouraged you to take a brief survey at the end of each session. The following few pages are simply longer versions of that short evaluation tool.

Your spiritual journey will take you to low spots as well as high places. Spiritual growth is not a smooth incline—a loopy roller coaster is more like it. When you regularly consider your life, you'll develop an awareness of God's Spirit working in you. Evaluate. Think. Learn. Grow.

The assessment in this section is a tool, not a test. The purpose of this tool is to help you evaluate where you are in your faith journey. No one is perfect, so don't worry about your score. It won't be published in your church bulletin. Be honest so you have an accurate idea of how you're doing.

When you finish, celebrate the areas where you're relatively healthy and think about how you can use your strengths to help others on their spiritual journeys. Then think of ways your group members can help one another to improve weak areas through support and example.

FELLOWSHIP: CONNECTING YOUR HEART TO OTHERS

1. I meet consistently with a small group of Christians.

1	2	3	4	5
POOR				OUTSTANDING

2. I'm connected to other Christians who hold me accountable.

1	2	3	4	5
POOR				OUTSTANDING

3. I can talk with my small group leader when I need help, advice, or support.

1	2	3	4	5
POOR				OUTSTANDING

4. My Christian friends are a significant source of strength and stability in my life.

1	2	3	4	5
POOR				OUTSTANDING

5. I regularly pray for others in my small group outside of our meetings.

1	2	3	4	5
POOR				OUTSTANDING

6. I have resolved all conflicts with other people—both Christians and non-Christians.

1	2	3	4	5
POOR				OUTSTANDING

7. I've done all I possibly can to be a good son or daughter and brother or sister.

1	2	3	4	5
POOR				OUTSTANDING

TOTAL:_____

Take time to answer the following questions to further evaluate your spiritual health. You can do this after your small group meets if you don't have time during the meeting. If you need help with this, schedule a time with your small group leader to talk about your spiritual health.

8. List the three most significant relationships you have right now. Why are these people important to you?

9. How would you describe the benefit from being in fellowship with other Christians?

10. Do you have an accountability partner? If so, what have you been doing to hold each other accountable? If not, how can you get one?

DISCIPLESHIP: GROWING TO BE LIKE JESUS

11. I have regular times of conversation with God.

1	2	3	4	5
POOR				OUTSTANDING

12. I'm closer to God this month than I was last month.

1	2	3	4	5
POOR				OUTSTANDING

13. I'm making better decisions this month compared to last month.

1	2	3	4	5
POOR				OUTSTANDING

14. I regularly attend church services and grow spiritually as a result.

1	2	3	4	5
POOR				OUTSTANDING

15. I consistently honor God with my finances through giving.

1	2	3	4	5
POOR				OUTSTANDING

16. I regularly study the Bible on my own.

1   2   3   4   5
POOR   OUTSTANDING

17. I regularly memorize Bible verses or passages.

1   2   3   4   5
POOR   OUTSTANDING

TOTAL:_____

Take time to answer the following questions to further evaluate your spiritual health. You can do this after your small group meets if you don't have time during the meeting. If you need help with this, schedule a time with your small group leader to talk about your spiritual health.

18. What books or chapters from the Bible have you read during the last month?

19. What has God been teaching you lately from Scripture?

20. What was the last verse you memorized? When did you memorize it? Describe the last time a memorized Bible verse helped you.

MINISTRY: SERVING OTHERS IN LOVE

21. I am currently serving in some ministry capacity.

1	2	3	4	5
POOR				OUTSTANDING

22. I'm effectively ministering where I'm serving.

1	2	3	4	5
POOR				OUTSTANDING

23. Generally I have a humble attitude when I serve others.

1	2	3	4	5
POOR				OUTSTANDING

24. I understand God has created me as a unique individual, and he has a special plan for my life.

1	2	3	4	5
POOR				OUTSTANDING

25. When I help others, I typically don't look for anything in return.

1	2	3	4	5
POOR				OUTSTANDING

26. My family and friends consider me generally unselfish.

1	2	3	4	5
POOR				OUTSTANDING

27. I'm usually sensitive to others' hurts and respond in a caring way.

1	2	3	4	5
POOR				OUTSTANDING

TOTAL:_____

Take time to answer the following questions to further evaluate your spiritual health. You can do this after your small group meets if you don't have time during the meeting. If you need help with this, schedule a time with your small group leader to talk about your spiritual health.

28. If you're currently serving in a ministry, why are you serving? If not, what's kept you from getting involved?

29. What spiritual lessons have you learned while serving?

30. What frustrations have you experienced as a result of serving?

EVANGELISM: SHARING YOUR STORY AND GOD'S STORY

31. I regularly pray for my non-Christian friends.

1	2	3	4	5
POOR				OUTSTANDING

32. I invite my non-Christian friends to church.

1	2	3	4	5
POOR				OUTSTANDING

33. I talk about my faith with others.

1	2	3	4	5
POOR				OUTSTANDING

34. I pray for opportunities to share what Jesus has done in my life.

1	2	3	4	5
POOR				OUTSTANDING

35. People know I'm a Christian because of what I do, not just because of what I say.

1	2	3	4	5
POOR				OUTSTANDING

36. I feel strong compassion for non-Christians.

1	2	3	4	5
POOR				OUTSTANDING

37. I have written my testimony and am ready to share it.

1	2	3	4	5
POOR				OUTSTANDING

TOTAL:_____

Take time to answer the following questions to further evaluate your spiritual health. You can do this after your small group meets if you don't have time during the meeting. If you need help with this, schedule a time with your small group leader to talk about your spiritual health.

38. Describe any significant spiritual conversations you've had with non-Christians during the last month.

39. Have non-Christians ever challenged your faith? If yes, describe how.

40. Describe some difficulties you've faced when sharing your faith.

41. What successes have you experienced recently in personal evangelism? (Success isn't limited to bringing people to salvation directly. Helping someone take a step closer at any point on his or her spiritual journey is success.)

WORSHIP: SURRENDERING YOUR LIFE TO HONOR GOD

42. I consistently participate in Sunday and midweek worship experiences at church.

1	2	3	4	5
POOR				OUTSTANDING

43. My heart breaks over the things that break God's heart.

1	2	3	4	5
POOR				OUTSTANDING

44. I regularly give thanks to God.

1	2	3	4	5
POOR				OUTSTANDING

45. I'm living a life that, overall, honors God.

1	2	3	4	5
POOR				OUTSTANDING

46. I have an attitude of wonder and awe toward God.

1	2	3	4	5
POOR				OUTSTANDING

47. I often use the free access I have into God's presence.

1   2   3   4   5

POOR   OUTSTANDING

TOTAL: _____

Take time to answer the following questions to further evaluate your spiritual health. You can do this after your small group meets if you don't have time during the meeting. If you need help with this, schedule a time with your small group leader to talk about your spiritual health.

48. Make a list of your top five priorities. You can get a good idea of your priorities by evaluating how you spend your time. Be realistic and honest. Are your priorities are in the right order? Do you need to get rid of some or add new priorities? (As a student you may have some limitations. This isn't ammo for dropping out of school or disobeying parents!)

49. List 10 things you're thankful for.

50. What influences, directs, guides, or controls you the most?

DAILY BIBLE READINGS

As you meet with your small group for Bible study, prayer, and encouragement, you'll grow spiritually. But no matter how wonderful your small group experience, you need to learn to grow spiritually on your own, too. God has given you an incredible tool to help—his love letter, the Bible. The Bible reveals God's love for you and gives directions for living life to the fullest.

To help you with this, we've included a fairly easy way to read through one of the Gospels. Instead of feeling like you need to sit down and read the entire book at once, we've broken down the reading into bite-size chunks. Check off the passages as you read them. Don't feel guilty if you miss a daily reading. Simply do your best to develop the habit of being in God's Word daily.

A 30-Day Journey Through the Gospel of Luke

Imagine sitting at the feet of Jesus himself: the Teacher who knows how to live life well, the Savior who died for you, the Lord who commands the universe. Like his first disciples, you can follow him around, watch what he does, listen to what he says, and pattern your life after his.

Day 1	Luke 1
Day 2	Luke 2
Day 3	Luke 3
Day 4	Luke 4
Day 5	Luke 5
Day 6	Luke 6:1–26
Day 7	Luke 6:27–49
Day 8	Luke 7:1–35
Day 9	Luke 7:36–50
Day 10	Luke 8:1–21
Day 11	Luke 8:22–56
Day 12	Luke 9:1–27
Day 13	Luke 9:28–62

Day 14   Luke 10

Day 15   Luke 11

Day 16   Luke 12:1–21

Day 17   Luke 12:22–59

Day 18   Luke 13

Day 19   Luke 14

Day 20   Luke 15

Day 21   Luke 16

Day 22   Luke 17

Day 23   Luke 18

Day 24   Luke 19

Day 25   Luke 20

Day 26   Luke 21

Day 27   Luke 22:1–38

Day 28   Luke 22:39–71

Day 29   Luke 23

Day 30   Luke 24

HOW TO STUDY THE BIBLE ON YOUR OWN

The Bible is the foundation for all the books in the EXPERIENCING CHRIST TOGETHER series. Every lesson contains a Bible passage for your small group to study and apply. To maximize the impact of your small group experience, it's helpful if each participant spends time reading and studying the Bible during the week. When you read the Bible for yourself, you can have discussions based on what *you* know the Bible says instead of what another member has heard second- or third-hand about the Bible.

Growing Christians learn to study the Bible so they can grow spiritually on their own. Here are some principles about studying the Bible to help you give God's Word a central place in your life.

Choose a Time and Place

Since we are easily distracted, pick a time when you're at your best. If you're a morning person, then study the Bible in the morning. Find a place away from phones, computers, and TVs so you are less likely to be interrupted.

Begin with Prayer

Acknowledge God's presence with you. Thank him for his gifts, confess your sins, and ask for his guidance and understanding as you study his love letter to you.

Start with Excitement

We often take God's Word for granted and forget what an incredible gift we have. God wasn't forced to reach out to us, but he did. He's made it possible for us to know him, understand his directions, and be encouraged—all through his Word, the Bible. Remind yourself how amazing it is that God wants you to know him.

Read the Passage

After choosing a passage, read it several times. You might want to read it slowly, pausing after each sentence. If possible, read it out loud. (Remember that before the Bible was written on paper, it was spoken verbally from generation to generation.)

Keep a Journal

Respond to God's Word by writing down how you're challenged, truths to remember, thanksgiving and praise, sins to confess, commands to obey, or any other thoughts you have.

Dig Deep

When you read the Bible, look deeper than the plain meaning of the words. Here are a few ideas about what to look for:

- *Truth about God's character.* What do the verses reveal about God's character?

- *Truth about your life and our world.* You don't have to figure out life on your own. Life can be difficult, but when you know how the world works, you can make good decisions guided by wisdom from God.

- *Truth about the world's past.* The Bible reveals God's intervention in our mistakes and triumphs throughout history. The choices we read about—good and bad—serve as examples to challenge us to greater faith and obedience. (See Hebrews 11:1-12:1.)

- *Truth about our actions.* God will never leave you stranded. Although he allows us all to go through hard times, he is always with us. Our actions have consequences and rewards. Just like he does in Bible stories, God can use all of the consequences and rewards caused by our actions to help others.

As you read, ask these four questions to help you learn from the Bible:

- What do these verses teach me about who God is, how he acts, and how people respond?

- What does this passage teach about the nature of the world?

- What wisdom can I learn from what I read?

- How should I change my life because of what I learned from these verses?

Ask Questions

You may be tempted to skip over parts you don't understand, but don't give up too easily. Understanding the Bible can be hard work. If you come across a word you don't know, look it up in a regular dictionary or a Bible dictionary. If you come across a verse that seems to contradict another verse, see whether your Bible has any notes to explain it. Write down your questions and ask someone who has more knowledge about the Bible than you. Buy or borrow a study Bible or check the Internet. Try *www.gotquestions.org* or *www.carm.org* for answers to your questions.

Apply the Truth to Your Life

The Bible should make a difference in your life. It contains the help you need to live the life God intended. Knowledge of the Bible without personal obedience is worthless and causes hypocrisy and pride. Take time to consider the condition of your thinking, attitudes, and actions, and wonder about how God is working in you. Think about your life situation and how you can serve others better.

More Helpful Ideas

- Decide that the time you have set aside for Bible reading and study is nonnegotiable. Don't let other activities squeeze Bible study time out of your schedule.

- Avoid the extremes of being ritualistic (reading a chapter just to mark it off a list) and being lazy (giving up).

- Begin with realistic goals and boundaries for your study time. If five to seven minutes a day proves a challenge at the beginning, make it a goal to start smaller and increase your time slowly. Don't set yourself up to fail.

- Be open to the leading and teaching of God's Spirit.

- Love God like he's the best friend you'll ever have—which is the truth!

MEMORY VERSES

The word *memory* may cause some of you to groan. In school, you have to memorize dates, places, times, and outcomes. Now you have to memorize the Bible?

No, not the entire Bible! Start small with some key verses. Trust us, this is important. Here's why: Scripture memorization is a good habit for a growing Christian to develop because when God's Word is planted in your mind and heart, it has a way of influencing how you live. King David understood this: "I have hidden your word in my heart that I might not sin against you" (Psalm 119:11).

Challenge one another in your small group to memorize the six verses below—one for each time your small group meets. Hold each other accountable by asking about one another's progress. Write the verses on index cards and keep them handy so you can learn and review them when you have a free moment (standing in line, before class starts, sitting at a red light, when you've finished a test and others are still working, waiting for your dad to get out of the bathroom—you get the picture). You'll be surprised at how many verses you can memorize as you work toward this goal and add verses to your list.

"HE WHO WALKS WITH THE WISE GROWS WISE, BUT A COMPANION OF FOOLS SUFFERS HARM." -PROVERBS 13:20

"A GENTLE ANSWER TURNS AWAY WRATH, BUT A HARSH WORD STIRS UP ANGER." -PROVERBS 15:1

"LET THE WORD OF CHRIST DWELL IN YOU RICHLY AS YOU TEACH AND ADMONISH ONE ANOTHER WITH ALL WISDOM, AND AS YOU SING PSALMS, HYMNS AND SPIRITUAL SONGS WITH GRATITUDE IN YOUR HEARTS TO GOD." -COLOSSIANS 3:16

"THEREFORE ENCOURAGE ONE ANOTHER AND BUILD EACH OTHER UP, JUST AS IN FACT YOU ARE DOING." -1 THESSALONIANS 5:11

"YOUR LOVE FOR ONE ANOTHER WILL PROVE TO THE WORLD THAT YOU ARE MY DISCIPLES." -JOHN 13:35 NLT

"BE KIND AND COMPASSIONATE TO ONE ANOTHER, FORGIVING EACH OTHER, JUST AS IN CHRIST GOD FORGAVE YOU." -EPHESIANS 4:32

JOURNALING: SNAPSHOTS OF YOUR HEART

In the simplest terms, journaling is reflection with pen in hand. A growing life needs time to reflect, so several times throughout this book you're asked to journal. In addition, you always have a journaling option at the end of each session. Through these writing opportunities, you're getting a taste of what it means to journal.

When you take time to write your thoughts in a journal, you'll experience many benefits. A journal is more than a diary—it's a series of snapshots of your heart. The goal of journaling is to slow down your life to capture some of the great, crazy, wonderful, chaotic, painful, encouraging, angering, confusing, joyful, and loving thoughts, feelings, and ideas in your life. Keeping a journal can become a powerful habit when you reflect on your life and how God is working in it.

Personal Insights

When confusion abounds in your life, disorderly thoughts and feelings often loom just out of range, slightly out of focus. Putting these thoughts and feelings on paper is like corralling and domesticating wild beasts. Once on paper, you can look at them, consider them, contemplate the reasons they were causing you pain, and learn from them.

Have you ever had trouble answering the question, "How do you feel?" Journaling compels you to become more specific with your generalized thoughts and feelings. This is not to suggest that a page full of words perfectly represents what's happening on the inside. That would be foolish. But journaling can move you closer to understanding more about yourself.

Reflection and Examination

With journaling, you can write about your feelings, your situations, how you responded to events. You can reflect and answer questions like these:

- Was that the right response?

- What were my other options?

- Did I lose control and act impulsively?

- If this happened again, should I do the same thing? Would I do the same thing?

- How can I be different as a result of this situation?

Spiritual Insights

One of the main goals of journaling is to gain new spiritual insights about God, yourself, and the world. When you take time to journal, you have the opportunity to pause and consider how God is working in your life and in the lives of those around you. Journaling helps you see the work he's accomplishing and remember it for the future.

What to Write About

There isn't one right way to journal, no set number of times per week, no rules for the length of each journal entry. Figure out what works best for you. Get started with these options:

Write a letter or prayer to God

Many Christians struggle with maintaining a consistent prayer life. Writing out your prayers can help strengthen it. Begin with this question: "What do I want to tell God right now?"

Write a letter or conversation to another person

Sometimes conversations with others can be difficult because we're not sure what we ought to say. Have you ever walked away from an interaction and 20 minutes later thought, *I should have said...*? Journaling conversations before they happen can help you think through the issues and approach your interactions with others in intentional ways. As a result, you can feel confident as you begin your conversations because you've taken time to consider the issues beforehand.

Process conflict and pain

You may find it helpful to write about your conflicts with others, especially those that take you by surprise. By journaling soon after conflict occurs, you can reflect and learn from it. You'll be better prepared for the next time you face a similar situation. Conflicts are generally difficult to navigate. Thinking through and writing about specific conflicts typically yields helpful personal insights.

When you're experiencing pain is also a good time to settle your thoughts and consider the nature of your feelings. The great thing about exploring your feelings is that you're only accountable to God. You don't have to worry about hurting anyone's feelings by what you write in your journal (if you keep it private).

Examine your motives

The Bible is clear regarding two heart truths. First, how you behave reflects who you are on the inside (Luke 6:45). Second, you can take the right action for the wrong reason (James 4:3).

The condition of your heart is vitally important. Molding your motives to God's desires is central to following Christ. The Pharisees did many of the right things, but for the wrong reasons. Reflect on the *real* reasons why you do what you do.

Anticipate your actions

Have you ever gone to bed thinking, *That was a mistake. I didn't intend that to happen!* Probably! No one is perfect. You can't predict all of the consequences of your actions. But reflecting on how your actions could affect others will guide you and help you relate better to others.

Reflect on God's work in your life

If you journal in the evening, you can answer this question: "What did God teach me today?"

If you journal in the morning, you can answer this question: "God, what were you trying to teach me yesterday that I missed?" When you reflect on yesterday's events, you may find a common theme that God may have been weaving into your life during the day—one you missed because you were busy. When you see God's hand in your life, even a day later, you know God loves you and is guiding you.

Record insights from Scripture

Journal about whatever you learn from the Bible. Rewrite a verse in your own words or figure out how a passage is structured. Try to uncover the key truths from the verses and see how the verses apply to your life. (Again, there is no right way to journal. The only wrong way is to not try it at all.)

JOURNAL PAGES

JOURNAL PAGES

JOURNAL PAGES

JOURNAL PAGES

JOURNAL PAGES

JOURNAL PAGES

PRAYING IN YOUR SMALL GROUP

As believers, we're called to support each other in prayer, and prayer should be a consistent part of a healthy small group.

One of prayer's purposes is aligning our hearts with God's. By doing this, we can more easily get in touch with what's at the center of God's heart. Prayer shouldn't be a how-well-did-I-do performance or a self-conscious, put-on-the-spot task to fear. Your small group may need time to get comfortable with praying out loud, too. That's okay.

When you do pray, silently or aloud, follow the practical, simple words of Jesus in Matthew 6:

Pray sincerely.

"And when you pray, do not be like the hypocrites, for they love to pray standing in the synagogues and on the street corners to be seen by men. I tell you the truth, they have received their reward in full." (Matthew 6:5)

In the Old Testament, God's people were disciplined prayer warriors. They developed specific prayers to use for every special occasion or need. They had prayers for light and darkness, prayers for fire and rain, prayers for good news and bad. They even had prayers for travel, holidays, holy days, and Sabbath days.

Every day the faithful would stop to pray at 9 a.m., noon, and 3 p.m.—a sort of religious coffee break. Their ritual was impressive, to say the least, but being legalistic had its downside. The proud, self-righteous types would strategically plan their schedules to be in the middle of a crowd when it was time for prayer so everyone could hear them as they prayed loudly. You can see the problem. What was intended to promote spiritual passion became a drama to impress others.

God wants our prayers addressed to him alone. That seems obvious enough, yet how many of us pray wanting to impress our listeners rather than wanting to truly communicate with God? This is the problem if you're prideful like the Pharisees about the excellent quality of your prayers. But it can also be a problem if you're new to prayer and are concerned that you don't know how to "pray right." Don't concern yourself with what others think; just talk to God as if you were sitting in a chair next to him.

Pray simply.

"And when you pray, do not keep on babbling like pagans, for they think they will be heard because of their many words. Do not be like them, for your Father knows what you need before you ask him." (Matthew 6:7-8)

God isn't looking to be dazzled with brilliantly crafted language. Nor is he impressed with lengthy monologues. It's freeing to know that he wants us to keep it simple.

Pray specifically.

"This, then, is how you should pray: 'Our Father in heaven, hallowed be your name, your kingdom come, your will be done on earth as it is in heaven. Give us today our daily bread. Forgive us our debts, as we also have forgiven our debtors. And lead us not into temptation, but deliver us from the evil one." (Matthew 6:9-13)

What the church has come to call "The Lord's Prayer" is a model of the kind of brief but specific prayers we may offer anytime, anywhere. Look at some of the specific items mentioned:

- Adoration: "hallowed be your name"

- Provision: "your kingdom come...your will be done...give us today our daily bread"

- Forgiveness: "forgive us our debts"

- Protection: "lead us not into temptation"

PRAYER REQUEST GUIDELINES

Because prayer time is so vital, group members need some basic guidelines for sharing, handling, and praying for prayer requests. Without a commitment from each person to honor these simple suggestions, prayer time can become dominated by one person, an opportunity to gossip, or a never-ending story time. (There are appropriate times to tell personal stories, but this may not be the best time.)

Here are a few suggestions for each group to consider:

Write down prayer requests.

Each small group member should write down every prayer request on the "Prayer Request" pages provided. When you commit to a small group, you're agreeing to be part of the spiritual community, and that includes praying for one another. By keeping track of prayer requests, you can see how God answers them. You'll be amazed at God's power and faithfulness.

As an alternative, one person can record the requests and e-mail them to the rest of the group. If your group chooses this option, safeguard confidentiality. Be sure personal information isn't compromised. Some people share e-mail accounts with parents or siblings. Develop a workable plan for this option.

Give everybody an opportunity to share.

As a group, consider the amount of time remaining and the number of people who still want to share. You won't be able to share every thought or detail about a situation.

Obviously if someone experiences a crisis, you may need to focus exclusively on that group member by giving him or her extended time and focused prayer. (However, true crises are infrequent.)

The leader can limit the time by making a comment such as one of the following:

- We have time for everyone to share one praise or request.

- Simply share what to pray for. We can talk in more detail later.

- We're only going to pray for requests about the people in our group. How can we pray for you specifically?

- We've run out of time to share prayer requests. Take a moment to write down your prayer request and give it to me [or identify another person]. You'll get them by e-mail tomorrow.

Just as people are free to share, they're free to not share.

The goal of a healthy small group should be to create an environment where participants feel comfortable sharing about their lives. Still, not everyone needs to share each week. Here's what I tell my small group:

> *As a small group we're here to support one another in prayer. This doesn't mean that everyone has to share something. In fact, don't assume you have to share at all. There's no need to make up prayer requests just to have something to say. If you have something you'd like the group to pray for, let us know. If not, that's fine, too.*

No gossip allowed.

Don't allow sharing prayer requests to become an excuse for gossip. If you're not part of the problem or solution, consider the information gossip. Share the request without the story behind it—that helps prevent gossip. Also speak in general terms without giving names or details ("I have a friend who's in trouble. God knows who it is. Pray for me that I can be a good friend.").

If a prayer request starts going astray, someone should kindly intercede, perhaps with a question such as, "How can we pray for you in this situation?"

Don't give advice or try to fix the problem.

When people share their struggles and problems, a common response is to try to fix the problem by offering advice. At the right time, the group might provide input on a particular problem, but during prayer time, keep focused on praying for the need. Often God's best work in a person's life comes through times of struggle and pain.

Keep in touch.

Make sure you exchange phone numbers and e-mail addresses before you leave the first meeting. That way you can contact someone who needs prayer or encouragement before the next time your group meets. You can write each person's contact information on the "Small Group Roster" (page 110).

PRAYER OPTIONS

There's no single, correct way to end all your sessions. In addition to the options provided in each session, here are some additional ideas.

During the Small Group Gathering

- One person closes in prayer for the entire group.

- Pray silently. Have one person close the silent prayer time after a while with "amen."

- The leader or another group member prays out loud for each person in the group.

- Everyone prays for one request or person. This can be done randomly during prayer or, as the request is shared, a willing person can announce, "I'll pray for that."

- Everyone who wants to pray takes a turn. Not everyone needs to pray out loud.

- Split the group in half and pray together in smaller groups.

- Pair up and pray for each other.

- On occasion, each person can share what he or she is thankful for before a prayer request, so prayer requests don't become negative from focusing only on problems. Prayer isn't just asking for stuff—it also includes praising God and being thankful for his generosity toward us.

- If you're having an animated discussion about a Bible passage or a life situation, don't feel like you must cut it short for prayer requests. Use it as an opportunity to add a little variety to the prayer time by praying some other day between sessions.

Outside the Group Time

You can use these options if you run out of time to pray during the meeting or in addition to prayer during the meeting.

- Send prayer requests to each other via e-mail.

- Pick prayer partners and phone each other during the week.

- Have each person in the small group choose a day to pray for everyone in the group. Perhaps you can work it out to have each day of the week covered. Let participants report back at each meeting for accountability.

- Have each person pray for just one other person in the group for the entire week. (Everyone prays for the person on the left or on the right or draw names.)

PRAYER REQUEST LOG

DATE	NAME	REQUEST	ANSWER

PRAYER REQUEST LOG

DATE | NAME | REQUEST | ANSWER

PRAYER REQUEST LOG

DATE	NAME	REQUEST	ANSWER

PRAYER REQUEST LOG

DATE

NAME

REQUEST

ANSWER

PRAYER REQUEST LOG

DATE	NAME	REQUEST	ANSWER

PRAYER REQUEST LOG

DATE

NAME

REQUEST

ANSWER

EXPERIENCING CHRIST TOGETHER FOR A YEAR

Your group will benefit the most if you work through the entire EXPERIENC-ING CHRIST TOGETHER series. The longer your group is together, the better your chances of maturing spiritually and integrating the biblical purposes into your life. Here's a plan to complete the series in one year.

Begin with a planning meeting and review the books in the series. They are:

Book 1—Beginning in Jesus: Six Sessions on the Life of Christ

Book 2—Connecting in Jesus: Six Sessions on Fellowship

Book 3—Growing in Jesus: Six Sessions on Discipleship

Book 4—Serving Like Jesus: Six Sessions on Ministry

Book 5—Sharing Jesus: Six Sessions on Evangelism

Book 6—Surrendering to Jesus: Six Sessions on Worship

We recommend you begin with *Book 1—Beginning in Jesus: Six Sessions on the Life of Christ,* because it contains an introduction to six qualities of Jesus. After that, you can use the books in any order that works for your particular ministry.

As you look at your youth ministry calendar, you may want to tailor the order in which you study the books to complement events your youth group will experience. For example, if you plan to have an evangelism outreach, study *Book 5—Sharing Jesus: Six Sessions on Evangelism* first to build momentum. Or study *Book 4—Serving Like Jesus: Six Sessions on Ministry* in late winter to prepare for the spring break missions trip.

Use your imagination and celebrate the completion of each book. Have a worship service, an outreach party, a service project, a fun night out, a meet-the-family dinner, or whatever else you can dream up.

Number of Weeks	Meeting Topic
1	Planning meeting—a casual gathering to get acquainted, discuss expectations, and refine the covenant (page 18).
6	Beginning in Jesus: Six Sessions on the Life of Christ
1	Celebration
6	Connecting in Jesus: Six Sessions on Fellowship
1	Celebration
6	Growing in Jesus: Six Sessions on Discipleship
1	Celebration
6	Serving Like Jesus: Six Sessions on Ministry
1	Celebration
6	Sharing Jesus: Six Sessions on Evangelism
1	Celebration
6	Surrendering to Jesus: Six Sessions on Worship
1	Celebration
2	Christmas Break
1	Easter Break
6	Summer Break

ABOUT THE AUTHORS

A youth ministry veteran of 25 years, **Doug Fields** has authored or co-authored more than 40 books, including *Purpose-Driven® Youth Ministry* and *Your First Two Years in Youth Ministry*. With an M.Div. from Fuller Theological Seminary, Doug is a teaching pastor and pastor to students at Saddleback Church in Southern California and president of Simply Youth Ministry. He and his wife, Cathy, have three children.

Brett Eastman has served as the leader of small groups for both Willow Creek Community Church and Saddleback Church. Brett is now the founder and CEO of LIFETOGETHER, a ministry whose mission is to "transform lives through community." Brett earned his masters of divinity degree from Talbot School of Theology and lives in Southern California.

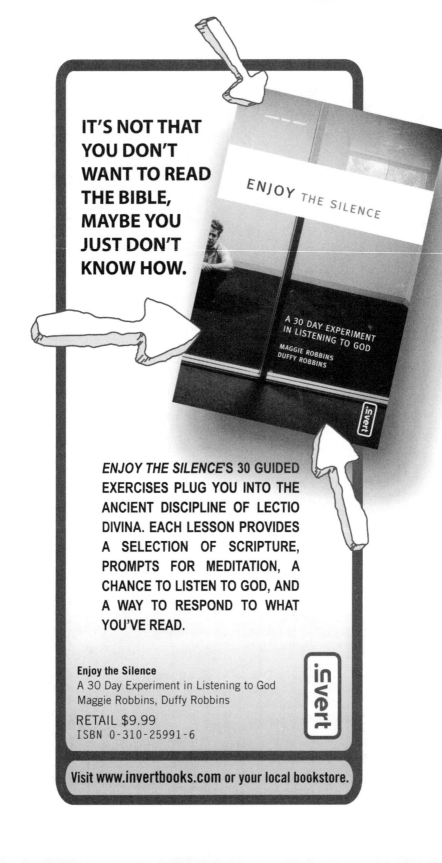

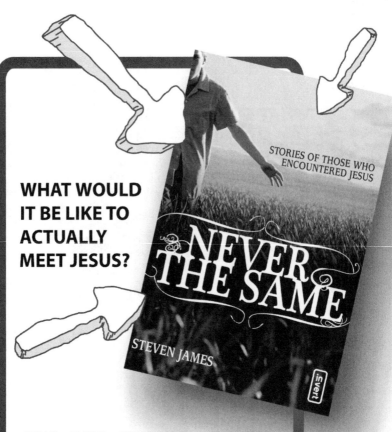